DEALING WITH LIFE WHEN IT HURTS

CR BOONSTRA

Gotham Books

30 N Gould St.
Ste. 20820, Sheridan, WY 82801
https://gothambooksinc.com/

Phone: 1 (307) 464-7800

© 2024 *CR Boonstra*. All rights reserved.

No part of this book may be reproduced, stored in a retrieval system, or transmitted by any means without the written permission of the author.

Published by Gotham Books (August 21, 2024)

ISBN: 979-8-3303-5483-2 (H)
ISBN: 979-8-3302-8111-4 (P)
ISBN: 979-8-3302-8112-1 (E)

Because of the dynamic nature of the Internet, any web addresses or links contained in this book may have changed since publication and may no longer be valid.

The views expressed in this work are solely those of the author and do not necessarily reflect the views of the publisher, and the publisher hereby disclaims any responsibility for them.

CONTENTS

DEDICATION v

PROLOGUE vi

WHAT IS HAPPENING? 1

WHAT IS HURT?... 13

MY STORY 20

CONNECTIONS.. 31

HOW THE HURTING FEEL 40

WHY ME, WHY NOT?... 53

MERE WORDS... 66

DON'TS 74

DO'S 81

ADJUSTMENTS.. 93

PERSONAL CONFLICT... 103

PERSPECTIVE 115

INTRIGUING WORDS 129

NUTSHELL 143

DEDICATION

This book is dedicated first and foremost to my Savior Jesus Christ. Then to all the people who are dealing with the negative things that this challenging, and non-respective world they live in subjects them to.

PROLOGUE

Life is fragile. It cannot be put on hold but must be lived despite its susceptibility to malfunction and disappointment. We only get one and by the time we figure out what we want to do with it, it's over.

Regardless of how, where, or when we live, things don't always go as planned. When the bottom falls out or something unexpected happens, we go from denial to acceptance only to realize we don't know what to expect or do. Our natural instinct is survival, to hang on or just get through while trying to maintain dignity and normalcy.

Anybody that has endured anything from a disappointment to a major setback knows about emotions, needs, relationships and choices. When unplanned or unexpected things happen, our lives must change. Most of us don't like this kind of change because not only are we unprepared, but it's usually not on our terms.

Although we try putting problems into a box to make things work in a uniform fashion, it rarely works. We are all unique in our personalities, emotions, priorities, and abilities. Followed by our environment, culture, age, gender, convictions, and those who have a direct influence upon us.

Once we get past the pride and seek wisdom from those who have already endured and learned, we usually find not only common ground of a particular situation, but also a bond of understanding. Life is about relationships and maturity. A journey that comes in the form of many changes, choices, and the time we are allowed to have or make an impact on those around us.

It is neither wrong nor shameful in seeking help to improve life. It matters not what has contributed to where you are now. What matters, is you making the choice to move on in life.

Somewhere in our subconscious, we have gotten the idea we need to suppress or ignore certain feelings and emotions that come during times of difficulty. Wrong, these human expressions are ways of dealing with life. It does not mean you're weak, it means you're normal.

WHAT IS HAPPENING?

Worried due to the circumstance you feel unjustly subjected to? Is fear of the unknown wrapping you in a blanket of more questions than answers? You probably feel alone, humiliated, unprepared, inadequate, judged by others, and challenged beyond your abilities.

Life can be overwhelming when it seems everything goes wrong or works against us. We may even feel cheated because of the abilities we have compared to those around us. Our idea or plan of what life should be fails, and we find ourselves depending on others. If we are not self-sufficient and able to function normally in society, we tend to downgrade ourselves to the point of feeling useless. We become convinced in our minds, that life as an unproductive person is too difficult, and we have become nothing less than a burden to those around us.

It has been said that everybody has a story to tell, but it seems hard to find anybody that really cares to listen, or to come along beside us for support when our burdens overwhelm.

As soon as I tell you it need not be that way, you will probably mentally flip the off switch, sarcastically saying to yourself what does this guy know? He has no idea what I've been dealing with, he's not living my life. How can he relate to my circumstance?

First I must tell you I was right where you are. I could not write this if I did not experience the exact things I just described. As I write this I am still in the middle of the trial God has allowed in my life. I do not see a way for this to end in a good, or timely manner from my limited human point of view.

I am not a person of credentials and book knowledge telling you what the practical answer is. It is only by the experience of personally dealing with life, that I hopefully am able to encourage and help you understand the emotional roller coaster of unknowns, and unwanted problems that YOU are personally subjected to.

Correct, I do not know your circumstance, but I do know we are all the same. It doesn't matter if we are of a certain ethnic background, man, woman, rich, poor, or any other thing that may define who we are personally. We were all created by God, are born, breathe air, have red blood, and eventually die.

Life isn't: Always sunshine, never a negative moment, everything is easy fairy-tale. Without a doubt we will all face times of uncertainty, difficult challenges, and the need to deal with changes we never intended to.

It is during these times we feel the hurts of life. Most of us are unprepared, and quickly come to the point of desperately wanting someone to give us comfort through words of encouragement, or a shoulder to lean on.

Depending on your personality and maturity, the potholes of life can and will influence or affect you differently than others. Other contributing factors of influence can be: Age, health, environment, relationships, locations, resources, and those close to you.

I believe there are basically four different types of hurting situations in life. We are not exempt from having to endure more than one, sometimes at the same time, and sometimes multiple times. The four types are:

1. Emotional
2. Physical
3. Financial
4. Spiritual

Hurting people sometimes feel they are in a prison, locked in a world that others cannot penetrate or relate to. Something came into their life, shattering what was once a calm comfortable satisfactory way of life. Now they feel set aside from the normal routines. An outsider, who wants desperately to turn back time and return to the familiar routines of the past, initially we tell ourselves it can't be happening, these things only happen to other people. I don't deserve this, I'm a good person. Eventually we must acknowledge and accept the fact, that whatever is happening must now be dealt with. We can't go back or ignore what has taken place, so once reality has set in, we must make personal choices and adjustments in our lives to include the changes.

When our ship finally comes in we find ourselves at the airport, isn't that how life goes? We always seem to be in the wrong place at the wrong time. Things don't happen as we think they should and we feel life has somehow treated us unfairly, especially when we did everything right and should be rewarded instead of penalized.

All that having been said, let me tell you there is hope! Our creator God cares for you as an individual, yes YOU. Each one of us is important to God. I will try to show you what I have learned, and hopefully encourage you in your pursuit of living a God honoring life.

Before you pass judgment on where I am heading or think I'm simply going to give the expected answers, like think positive and everything will work out. I wish to tell you from my own experience, that when things go sour all the rules are out the window! We are made with emotions, personalities, desires, and needs. When life is out of balance we fall down and it hurts. Getting back up takes time, effort, and sometimes help.

I must make one thing perfectly clear. I believe the Bible (Gods word) is not only a guidebook, but also the final authority pertaining to what choices we should make concerning the struggles we may have throughout life. I will also inject a disclaimer by saying, when things are upside down, foggy or confusing, the front door of having a perfect answer that fits every situation is absurd. A backdoor approach with the same result is sometimes necessary, always with a goal of restoring individual lives and relationships, to understanding acceptance and contentment.

When things go wrong or different than what we consider logical or right, we begin to self-judge, allowing thoughts of worthlessness and self-pity to creep in. We need to stop beating ourselves up in this manner before we actually start believing it. Desiring improvement of circumstance to make our lives better is NOT wrong.

Regardless of what the hurt is, because you are the one directly involved, it is the worst possible situation to deal with. The degree of difficulty or hurt, is directly related to how involved YOU as an individual are.

Sometimes in our frustration we need someone to put our feelings into the right words. You know the feelings but are unable to express it to the ones closest to you. We all need help at times, maybe due to embarrassment, possible misunderstanding, or you're just too tired from the events that brought you to this point in life. May this book be the aid, help or insight you have longed to find. Bridging the gap between feelings, communication, and getting others to understand your pain. May it also help you connect with those involved in your life as it exposes some of the underlying reasons we react as we do in uncharted, unwanted, life altering circumstances.

Ecclesiastes is a book of the bible written by Solomon, the wisest man who ever lived. He elaborates on the theme of how short and senseless life can be. How everything is the same from generation to generation, and how things don't always happen in the logical way we think it should. Job 14:1, sums up mans life on this earth. "Man born of woman, is of few days and full of trouble". The old saying, "The more things change, the more they stay the same," is dripping with truth. The simple application is that we are no different than anybody who has lived before us. So hang in there, persevere, continue on, keep your eye on the goal (eternity with God) don't ever give up! God is in control and has a plan for you, even when things have a bleak outlook.

This book is not just for the hurting. It is also for those who genuinely desire to understand, and be a support to those going through difficult situations in life.

Hurting is very real, but sometimes people hide it so others cannot see. Most people who hurt actually withdraw from telling even those close to them how they really feel, possibly for fear of being misunderstood, or the fear of being judged. Humans are proud and generally don't want to expose ourselves as one who might be weak enough to need the help or support of others.

When someone is hurt physically, they go to the doctor or hospital to get help. Depending on the severity of the wound or infliction is the amount of time, type of treatment, or medicine required for proper healing. When people hurt in non-physical ways, due to life bringing undesirable situations, they also need time and the right type of treatment to heal and recover. We cannot expect them to just get on with life as if nothing happened.

So where do those who are hurting in ways other than the physical go for healing? There are multiple verses in the book of Proverbs telling us to seek council or wisdom. I believe God is telling us we need to seek out those around us who can give insight, possibly from experience or training concerning whatever the issue is we may need guidance with. It is so much easier to make a good decision or choice if we have researched our options.

The common phrase "out of sight, out of mind," is one many of us embrace and practice, simply because we do not know what to do. So rather than offend someone, we avoid them. In our own mind we believe we have done them a favor, but the reality is we have done just the opposite by making them believe they are unimportant and not worth our efforts. Consequently from their viewpoint, the gap in the relationship has widened regardless of good intentions.

May any and all words of this book be taken in the right context and understanding. My sincere desire here is to inform, encourage, and lift up those who are dealing with difficult situations or circumstances in life. It is no secret that trials in life, have the ability to discourage or even ruin a relationship with God and man. Life is about choices, relationships, and maturing, may we all come to the point of making a positive decision to encourage each other unconditionally. May we also be humble enough to allow others to come beside us when they are needed, simply because together there is not only encouragement, but strength.

It certainly would be nice if there were a list of steps we could go through, that would bring guaranteed relief in a timely manner if followed correctly. God is the only guarantee we have, and his word is the guide. First we need to comprehend, acknowledge, and gain the understanding that every person is unique and that the difficulties of life do not work in a cookie cutter manner with emotional beings. Even children in the same family living in the same environment, will act and react differently to their surroundings. People as a rule are not all the same and will react differently to the same type of situation because of personalities, demeanors, conscience and understanding. Hopefully with the right motivation, attitude and choices, the result or outcome will shape them into who God wants them to be.

When you or someone you know is dealing with one of lifes hurts, trials, or an undesired circumstance, we automatically assume that whoever is involved including ourselves, must have done something to bring the present situation upon them. That is possible but not always the case. Please don't judge or jump to a conclusion without knowing all the details or facts.

It is not our place to judge, but to love unconditionally. Somebody may have done everything right and still can be a victim of circumstance. To backup that claim up, I reference 2 Samuel chapter 11 where Uriah, Bathsheba's husband was killed because of David's sin. Solomon also informs us in Ecclesiastes 9:11 "The race is not to the swift or the battle to the strong, nor does food come to the wise, wealth to the brilliant, or favor to the learned: But time and chance happen to them all".

If you have lived on the earth for any length of time, you will have learned that the results desired are not always what comes to be. One might even say to expect the unexpected.

We all live in the same place, and are susceptible to the same types of issues, regardless of who we are as told to us in Matthew 5:45 "He causes his sun to rise on the evil and the good, and sends rain on the righteous and the unrighteous".

Another argument or disagreement some may wish to express, is how God hates the bad or negative attitude and by dwelling therein someone may be committing sin. Suffering or the emotions that go with it do not equal sin. God gave us these emotions and he tells us in Ecclesiastes chapter three there is a time for all of them. Just because someone is dealing with difficult issues or a storm in life and may express the negative things that accompany it, does not mean they have the wrong attitude or are committing sin. They most likely are trying to sum up what has happened, how it changes things and what direction to take next. We live in a world where things do go wrong, and we need to acknowledge the bad before we can put it in proper perspective.

This book will bring out many negative things and I would rather dwell on the positive. However we need to explore the negative aspects of shattered lives to understand how they influence us. Only then can we make informed decisions for the positive results we desire. I don't believe God wants us to hide our heads in the sand of ignorance. I'm sure you did not sign up or volunteer for whatever the issue is you are dealing with. God is not a God of confusion but a God of peace, and if you are reading this book it's probably because you desire that peace.

Many things we have or enjoy during our time on this earth, may be taken away and without warning. Materialistic things or the stuff we desire for personal satisfaction. Relationships can change or be strained through death, distance or some other circumstance. Even our physical abilities may change due to age or some unforeseen incident. Your life may have hit a brick wall and come to an abrupt halt, stuck for the moment in uncertainty, you may be frustrated as you try to make decisions with inadequate information or experience.

However hope cannot be taken away. Hope is belief in something or someone. Never convince yourself or believe there is no hope. Don't ever quit or give up trying. Hope is what gives us stamina, drive, and a reason to press on. Hope means there is always a chance or possibility for something or someone to change. As long as you are alive, there is hope!

WHAT IS HURT?

It is imperative to explore the meaning or have an explanation of what hurt is, thus helping us understand when we are actually dealing with it. The logical place to go for this revelation is a dictionary, which hopefully gives us a broader understanding of clarity and meaning.

The dictionary definition of hurt is a negative effect. It can be in the form of pain, setbacks, or some other sort of difficulty, causing us to experience something undesirable or unpleasant.

My personal definition of hurt, is when we are plunged into a chaotic, uncontrollable, unknown circumstance. It can include pain, both physical and emotional, loneliness, uncertainty, inadequacy, inability, and even misunderstandings.

The degree of suffering a hurt, or how much impact it has on us can be as broad as the world is big. Sometimes tolerable like a small irritation or scratch, sometimes so severe it dominates our whole being. The severity of an unpleasant circumstance seems to amplify with time. The longer it drags on, the more severe it become in our minds. If it doesn't last very long we find it tolerable and easier to forget about or live with. However if it continues for a period of extended time or comes with more pain and sorrow, our natural human nature tends to embrace a negative attitude. We as humans have a bent towards dwelling more on the negative things that surround us than on the positive. This is really a backwards or wrong approach to changing our outlook. Good or positive things are always there even in our darkest times. We tend to overlook them, believing they have somehow lost their value in comparison to what a storm in life is overwhelming us with.

Everybody can come up with a few examples, of how he or she has been hurt or had to deal with trials at sometime during their life, and the results of how it has influenced or changed them, good or bad. Yes there are scars, but those are to remind us later what we've been through, lest we forget the decisions and change of priorities we may have made during those detours. Trials, hurt, unplanned or undesirable situations that disrupt our *normal* lives, can come at anytime during life. We never grow out of the possibility or become exempt with age, status, wealth, or even maturity.

The four basic categories or reasons people hurt:

1. **Physical**: Physical is generally associated with the human body. Our strength or abilities to function. Sometimes things come into our physical lives that cause us to be less functional. We are not all created with the same physical characteristics. We differ

in sex, abilities, and size. We are all made unique and it's possible we are affected differently by the same situation. Some people are born with physical problems, or something in life just happens that can change them in a manner where they must deal with a bodily issue for the rest of our life. Our physical pain or trial whether short or long term, can also have implications in other areas of who we are, by the way we choose to emotionally handle the disruption or change that has occurred.

2. **Financial**: Financial refers to our ability to buy sell or manage our resources, in order to provide for our needs or wants. Basically we have a certain amount of money or resources to work with, and we try to adjust our lifestyle and goals to work within those means. However we all know only to well that things don't always go as planned. A financial hardship may come because of some physical need. Maybe an accident, divorce, family, house, gambling, death, job, or even the possibility you made some bad decisions and now need to live with the consequences. Things tend to need fixing or be replaced at what we consider the worst possible times. The list of financial needs or

hardships, can be as long or varied as there are people on this earth.

3. **Emotional**: Emotions are feelings or opinions through reasoning with whatever information we have accumulated. Emotions can be swayed or challenged by outside influences. Our emotions are directly influenced by what life has dealt us, and certainly by those we associate with. Low self-esteem, despair, broken relationships and loneliness are heavy burdens that can directly affect our emotions. The most important point I wish to make about emotions is the attitude that accompanies it. We all experience different emotions as life happens, however, I believe we choose the attitude regardless of the emotion a situation brings, and that attitudes influence is greater than the emotion.

4. **Spiritual**: The spirit is the heart, soul, and mind. The connection to the religious or sacred things of life, our core beliefs, our inner being or will, non materialistic. The important challenge is to know who God, the ultimate supreme spiritual being is. Having a genuine relationship with him, allows us to stand strong during trying times. When things go awry you probably question what

truth is, what you really believe is truth, and if there are absolutes. The spiritual is the core of what you believe life is based on through faith and hope, the unseen principles of what allows things to exist and function.

Each one of these four areas can bring a hurt or difficulty so severe, it can dominate our entire being. As much as we don't want to admit it or even bring the discussion up. There are times of despair when we all may entertain thoughts of giving up or quitting because it's just to hard, or we convince ourselves it doesn't make any difference anyway. It is not wrong to evaluate your life. If we never took stock of who we were or what our priorities are, we eventually became a society of directionless robots.

The important factor during these times of personal evaluations and conviction, is not that we are thinking about them, but the decision to make choices with the right attitude and motivation, allowing God to use whatever our situation is for his glory.

During times of hurt or personal struggles, we make choices that are usually based on protecting ourselves. Such as ending a relationship for physical or emotional reasons, or we may become selfish with the money and resources we have, justifying it with the me first I've earned it attitude. In the spiritual we become easily frustrated when things we have prayed for or believed in, have different results than we expected or hoped for.

The deeper one gets into something the harder it is to get back out. The tendency in extreme cases is to avoid those people, lest we be somehow sucked into it and feel the pain, sorrow, or get hurt ourselves. Those are the times the hurting person needs someone to willingly come along side, to share the burden in an unconditional nonjudgmental manner, regardless of what choices they may have made previously or how they got there in the first place. What if you were the one who needed a shoulder to lean on?

Life's detours, interruptions, and difficulties that cause hurt, pain, and disappointment, are to numerous to name. Obviously I can't name everything (I'd probably miss your particular misfortune if I tried). But I think we can agree all hurts and circumstances are not the same. They come in varying degrees of difficulty and timelines. Sometimes we may even experience more than one type of hurt or hardship at the same time, and usually do. For instance, someone is sick and the hospital bills add up, causing not only physical and financial difficulty, but maybe put strain on the emotional and spiritual at the same time.

We may not be able to control the physical, or financial, but I strongly believe we make our choices when it comes to the emotional and the spiritual. Choices to have the right attitude, seek and acknowledge God, give him our burdens and submit to his will. Yes, there are some emotional diseases that need medical help, but most of us can't use that excuse.

One thing is for sure. Nobody is exempt from feeling some kind of hurt during his or her lifetime, both directly and indirectly. We live in a sinful world full of uncertainty, disillusions, pain, sorrow, and death. Hurts can come in the form of one thing or many. It can vary in degrees of difficulty and may be of short endurance or a lifetime of challenges. Whatever or whenever things come that challenge and disrupt our comfortable world, we need to look at them as opportunities to grow in maturity, while accepting the changes with the right attitude.

MY STORY

Back to the phrase suggested in the first chapter, everybody has a story to tell. Although that is a true statement no story is really complete until the end of life. Our lives are full of little stories, or chapters that together make up our entire story. Even after your life has ended in death, the story continues with each person you have touched during your time on this earth.

What kind of legacy do you wish to leave? What will those who know you now, say about you? Are you content with their answer to that question? I sincerely hope not, because God uses words like: Seek, go, persevere, never telling us we have arrived or have the right to quit. So your story regardless of where you are now, is only partially complete. All of us for long as we live are in a continuous process of becoming who we are.

All right, I know you are probably asking what my trial is, and how God brought me to this point in my life. Again I wish to make it perfectly clear – I am a child of the king through Jesus Christ my savior, and the only reason I wish to tell my story is to encourage and let others know, they are not alone or the only one. The reason for writing down these thoughts, are not only to help those hurting but especially to inform those who desire to help, understand the feelings, thoughts, motivations, and how God may want you to fit into the picture.

I realize my particular type of endurance or trial may not be the same as yours, and I certainly don't pretend to know how you feel. I do know the principles are the same as we deal with emotions and relationships. I make no claims to be any wiser or more educated than you. I hold no official degree. My only credentials are life's experiences and Gods leading. I am just an ordinary normal average guy who went to the school of hard knocks. I acknowledge my shortcomings and realize I still have much to learn.

Now that I have opened myself to criticism for lack of training or education, I wish to express why I exposed myself in such a manner.

Some people will not respect or listen, to the advice or insights of someone who has a degree or holds some type of rank beyond where they are in life. Sometimes we have a tendency to feel those with book knowledge or credentials, only have the generic answers without practical experience. Maybe its pride or possibly a preconceived notion, that someone with all the right credentials cannot relate. The gap between the two groups in communication and applicable solutions can be a deterrent even before trying to find solutions.

Therefore, if I help one person just by being who I am, my efforts and time are worthwhile. I must inject a disclaimer here, I know God is not a respecter of persons and we are all the same before him. I also know as humans, we do feel and even place ourselves in different classes or levels. I'm not trying to justify it, but expose how the society we live in pushes certain ideas of respect or ability to relate. Hopefully I can help you see beyond yourself through my experience, to understand how we all need support in life at sometime. As I have experienced over the past few months, I can wholeheartedly confirm, that when others come alongside in difficult times it creates a bond beyond understanding.

I wholeheartedly give proper respect to those who have spent the time and energy to educate themselves, hold degrees, or do things according to the book. The insights of these people are definitely worth researching and applying. We all need to be careful of judging others regardless of where we fit into society.

I have heard but have not personally experienced, that soldiers who have gone through some life challenging experience together have a bond like no other. It doesn't even matter if they are of the same religion, color, size, or sex, what matters is the understanding and dependency they have shared. They have built an unexpected relationship not necessarily of choice, but of circumstance and understanding.

God loves us and wants a relationship with us. He sometimes disciplines or allows things to disrupt our normal routines because he loves us and wants to have a deeper relationship. Lets be honest, sometimes we wish God didn't love us quite so much because those times of growing are not easy. It may not be a disciplinary measure you are experiencing, there are multiple reasons for the difficult seasons of our lives. It may be special training for a future opportunity God has in mind for you.

God only wants what is best for us and sometimes he allows things into our lives that we do not understand but are meant so we can grow closer to him. His plan for each of our lives as believers is to be more like Jesus. Just as we are born physically and grow into adulthood, we are born once again into Gods family by believing and accepting Christ as our savior.

Romans 10:9-10 "That if you confess with your mouth Jesus is Lord, and believe in your heart God raised him from the dead, you will be saved. For it is with your heart you believe and are justified, and it is with your mouth that you confess and are saved."

Once we experience that spiritual birth, we need to grow from babies into adulthood. Just like a tree needs strong roots to withstand the wind when it grows tall, we also need to have a firm foundation. Growing sometimes hurts but its with the growth that we become strong, and thus can be effective in life as in 2 Peter 1:5-8 which states:

"Make every effort to add to your faith goodness, and to goodness knowledge, and to knowledge self-control, and to self-control perseverance, and to perseverance godliness, and to godliness brotherly kindness, and to brotherly kindness, love. For if you possess these qualities in increasing measure, they will keep you from being ineffective and unproductive in your knowledge of the Lord Jesus Christ."

God got my attention by showing me he was in control and not me. He used the economic downturn as his tool to turn life upside down not only for me but also my life's partner, my wife of thirty plus years.

We had enjoyed approximately twenty years of good living, while I worked in the tool and die trade before I decided to venture out on my own.

I was self-employed in the metal working industry for eleven years before my world fell out from under me. Other than some farming experiences while growing up, tool and die was the only industry I had ever worked in.

Trying to build a future the American way, I had invested in industrial machinery and commercial real estate. We had even mortgaged our house to expand the business when the markets were in its boom.

Along with the major population in America I believed that with hard work, dedication and self-discipline, long-term financial goals could be achieved. With the rapid devaluation of most of these items over a period of only about a year, I was soon upside down in my debt to value ratio as many others can relate to.

It didn't take many months before the bank thought of me as a high risk, they stepped in forcing me to permanently close the doors of the business and lay off my four remaining employees. An auction followed where supply, demand, and depreciation, gave me nickels on the dollar.

At the same time manufacturing jobs disappeared at an alarming rate in the United States, especially in Michigan where we were located. Many other metal working shops in the area closed about the same time, adding scores of workers seeking employment. The only industry I really ever knew, in a sense had ceased to exist. Now there were only a fraction of the jobs that had existed just a few years ago, with most tooling work either going over seas or coming to a halt because of the economy lacking demand.

As an owner I was able to collect unemployment for only a couple of months. With jobs at a premium, I found myself in the position of being slightly older than most places desired to hire, and did not have a degree behind my name, which is required in most job markets today. I was only able to bring in minimal income by working part time and temporarily jobs.

In less than two years, my wife and I had lost everything materialistic we had worked for over the past thirty years. I did not have a full time job and the unemployment ran out. Additional stress came on me personally, because my wife had been a stay at home mom and depended on me for her financial needs. I felt I had let her down.

We changed our lifestyle to adjust to the lack of income. We had no steady income or health insurance for over a full year. We sold all our liquid assets trying to survive.

It is very hard to give up things and a life you are used to, not only due to the social class and the comforts or fulfillments that things give, but also the humility that comes with it. Maybe life was just too full of stuff, so God decided to relieve us of some worldly possessions, leaving room for his blessings.

Like many others, I had my hands so full God couldn't hold them or fill them. God wants us to hunger and thirst after him, not the material things of this disappointing world. The things we see are temporal and the things not seen are eternal. When disappointment or negative circumstances come into our lives, we make choices of priority and attitude. I encourage you to seek God and his will, not blame him and lose an opportunity to grow or be used by him.

When things looked bleak for my wife and I, one of the major efforts I made was to pray for wisdom. My concept of what wisdom was is to have enough common sense to make good choices. Only after enduring many days and months of disappointment and despair did I grasp what wisdom really is.

The definition of wisdom in the dictionary is the knowledge and experience needed to make sensible decisions. It was the and experience phase that I had not anticipated. The conclusion I soon drew was that some of the things I was enduring were a direct answer to my ignorant prayer. I was gaining the wisdom I prayed for through what I was experiencing. You see my prayers were answered but not the way I had anticipated, however I do feel blessed because of it. Now I feel I have gained some understanding as well as growing in the wisdom I prayed hard for.

Other things have also contributed to the hurts my wife and I have felt, however I hope I have told enough of my own demise to convince those reading, that this is not just a made up story so I have a reason to write a book. I really can relate to the emotional roller coaster of uncertainty and the disappointments that life brings. I also have had to make choices I thought I never would, and have learned to live by faith and depend on God. I know first hand what it feels like to be the recipient of other people's generosity, and the humility that comes with it.

Well that's my story so far, I'm not dead yet. Maybe you can relate to my story and are asking questions like, so now what? Is God really there and listening to our prayers? I assure you he is, I truly believe Romans 8:28 And we KNOW that in all things, God works for the good of those who love him, who have been called according to his purpose.

Don't misinterpret what is being said here. Work together for good does not necessarily mean our good, but for his purpose and glory. We need to let God use us unconditionally in the same way he loves us. I'm excited to share some thoughts, experiences, and spiritual lessons I have learned, and continue to learn. I know you are wondering if I have personally recovered from my demise. Some things have improved, while we still wrestle with other things, I choose to leave whatever life brings me in the hands of my God.

I do believe in hope because hope is of the lord. Most people who know me say I'm an optimist, always expecting the best. That's probably true, but only because I believe Gods word is true and I choose to live by faith with hope. Just knowing God cares for me, inspires me to never quit or give up on hope.

It's comforting, to find a passage in Gods word that helps fill the need of encouragement, or the desired peace for the difficulty we are presently experiencing in life.

One particular passage I have gone to has been Psalms chapters thirty-three and thirty-four. It reminds me to praise God because of who he is. I am encouraged when I read in his word that he knows and cares about me. It tells me God has not abandoned me, a great comfort during trying times. It also states what my responsibilities and privileges are in my relationship with God.

God uses average ordinary people for his glory if they have a right and willing heart. Sometimes we feel God is out there somewhere but not listening to our pleas for help. In Hebrews 13:5 he reminds us, "Be content with what you have, because God has said, never will I leave you, never will I forsake you".

God never leaves us, but we sometimes go off on our own for whatever reason. Just like relationships with other people we need to spend time with God to have a relationship, a true connection. We do this by reading his word and spending time alone in prayer with him.

Little prayer little power, some prayer some power, much prayer much power. James 5:16 "The prayer of a righteous man is powerful and effective". Communication with God is vital, but we must ask in Gods will and not for selfish gain. James 4:3 "When you ask you do not receive, because you ask with the wrong motives, that you may spend what you get on your own pleasures".

Prayer is the most important tool any believer has. I am disappointed when I hear a believer say "The least I can do is pray". Don't you realize that prayer is not the least, but the most!! That should be where we go first, it's direct excess to the creator of the universe with unlimited resources, the ultimate power who has the ability to help. Prayer is a tool that can be used on behalf of yourself or others, and I strongly urge for you to pray for each other first, whether you are the hurting or the helper.

I know my time with God has dramatically increased. I am very thankful for the disappointing things in life that have driven me toward a deeper relationship with my creator. He does take care of his own, he knows you better than you can imagine. Read Psalms chapter 139, it will give you a glimpse of who God is.

CONNECTIONS

It is almost impossible to live on this earth alone as the population grows and secluded areas disappear. We find our dependence to exist interconnected in multiple ways. Our supply lines to food, shelter, transportation, utilities or any other daily requirement to exist as we do, hinge on the services and abilities of others we may not even know. This world of existence is about relationships, dependence and doing our part.

Although we depend on each other for so much, things don't always work in the flawless manner we expect. Things break, accidents happens, personalities collide. When they do, someone suffers the consequences.

If you are the one hurting, typically one of the first types of questions or comments you express will be, where is God now? Why does he not answer my prayers? He seems to have abandoned me. I just don't feel his presence. Relax, you are normal when you ask these questions. You might question everything from your own responsibility, to how God fits into the present situation. If we did not have difficulties in our lives, do we become complacent, routine, or stuck in the rut of self-sufficiency?

A critical point in the process of dealing with the hurt, is for the hurting person to let others in. I know we have our pride and dignity. We certainly don't want others to know we may be weak or perish the thought, we just can't solve the problem on our own. We deceive ourselves when we think we can handle it alone, causing us to miss out on the benefits of having someone walk beside us.

Life is usually a series of steps when it comes to the unexpected interruptions in our structured routines. Initially when things get off the beaten path, we are self-confident and are usually able to fix things ourselves.

The next time it is slightly more complex or difficult, so we ask someone to come along side for both moral support and their ability or resources.

Then it may get even harder, but we somehow are still able make adjustments or change, possibly even a dramatic or drastic one to find a suitable solution, while maintaining control.

Finally the circumstance has deteriorated so far, it becomes obvious even to ourselves, that we are no longer in control. We can only cry out to God the supreme or ultimate power for help in our uncontrollable, humanly impossible to overcome situation of pain and hurt. Getting to the point of understanding our delicate position of dependence on God, can come quickly or take a lifetime, and sadly for some never.

I suggest we may just need a little push from the difficulties in life, forcing us not only to pursue God, but to reap the reward of a deeper relationship with him. We can and do become lazy, especially when it comes to acknowledging God in every aspect of our lives. As difficult as it is for most of us to admit, there are times in life we get comfortable or lazy where we are. We actually need a push from some outside circumstance to force us to mature or get out of our comfort zone.

Do you really believe there is a God? Without having some superior being to guide your life, are you at the mercy of chance? Is there purpose, reason or even a future to look forward to? You are an intelligent human, one who has the ability to think, reason, and make choices. If you do not have a relationship with the creator of all things seen and unseen, I challenge you to evaluate why not.

Let me ask a pointed question, do you personally know God and does he know you? We really can't expect God to help us if we don't have a relationship with him, can we? Are you anxious to help a complete stranger? Its a lot easier helping a friend, and we are usually willing to help a close family member even quicker. That's the picture, we have relationships with those we spend time with, and that should include God!

Having a relationship with God means: Admitting to God you are a sinner and asking for his forgiveness, acknowledge and believe that Jesus Christ died on the cross and rose from the grave for you, trusting Jesus to be your savior for all of eternity. Then like any other relationship you value, spend time with him!

The best part of having a genuine relationship with God, is that your guaranteed a place in heaven with God himself for all of eternity. Revelation 21:4 states: He will wipe every tear from their eyes, There will be no more death or mourning or crying or pain, for the old order of things has passed away!

Relationships take time! I'm not referring to the aspect of time in years but the time we spend daily. What if God gave you as much attention as you give him? Each one of us desires time with those we feel close to like our spouse, family member, or a friend. Those are the people who enrich our lives and give us a sense of belonging.

Sometimes an issue we are dealing with cannot be immediately resolved due to the timing. Like a seed planted in late fall will not grow or produce until the environment is right in the springtime. When we do not see immediate results or solutions to the present situation, our now generation attitude wants to give up hope. We willingly accept it when a doctor tells us the broken leg will take eight weeks to completely heal, but when it comes to other areas of life, we expect immediate results. We need to choose the right attitude regardless of the difficulty, along with the understanding that it's not all about what we think should happen, or when.

God is always there, we are the ones who choose to make or take the time with him. We should want to have constant communication and a growing relationship with him, like a parent, brother, sister, or close friend. Then when times of trouble come, you may rest in the assurance that he knows who you are, and desires to bring you through it as a child he loves and cares for. Notice I did say "through" not into. He wants us to complete or finish life with the goal of spiritual maturity. The hard part for us, is allowing God to be in control while going through the trials, difficulties, hardships, and hurts. Ultimately these things challenge us to grow into a mature believer for his purpose and glory, but when we are struggling through them, time drags and we want relief.

Self is usually our biggest enemy. We think we have all the answers along with the ability or resources to make it on our own. We take pride in being self-sufficient and certainly don't want to express any weakness or venerability by admitting we might fail.

Usually our first mistake because of pride, is not allowing anybody get close enough to give the needed input or help during times of personal weakness. We continue to walk aimless and hope for the best, thinking it can't be that bad, still convincing ourselves we can handle it alone.

Males probably deal with this factor more than females, simply due to the fact males have a tendency to think they are independent, self-sufficient, and invincible. Peer pressure sometimes pushes males to succeed no matter what, with the thought pattern of constant competition. Males are not just out to play the game, they are out to win. Failure makes them susceptible to the ridicule of other males. and is a major blow to their ego.

Generally speaking, males have very few close friends. They hardly ever open up with emotions or intimate feelings that might expose them as weak and not in control. The worlds view of what a man is or should be, does not allow for weakness or vulnerability. Men generally don't seek council, because to be a real man they must work it out on their own, maybe that's why we don't like to ask for directions. All decisions and actions come from whatever bits of information and other knowledge they have acquired in the past. Males like to base decisions on logic or what they see as practical, usually pushing emotions into the background.

Females generally have many friends, so they probably gather more information and get greater input this way. They also have the tendency to base their decisions on emotion more than logic. They are quicker to share things of the personal nature with other females, actually finding emotional support and strength to endure the hardship. They seem to be better communicators than males when it comes to difficulties in life.

These observations are not always the case as there are always exceptions. Because we all fit in the male female category, this information is nothing new to anybody. I'm simply giving a generalization to stimulate your thinking as to how we differ in our approach to life. We need to take as much information into account as possible to have a better understanding of how decisions are made. The more information and understanding we have of how everything involved influences us or the other person, allows us opportunity to make informed, wise, and helpful decisions the first time, instead of trial and error as is usually the case. That type of instinctive behavior usually adds to the frustration.

Hurts, regardless of what type it is, affect more than just the one individual involved. The best example to portray that is marriage. When two people live shared lives, there really is no separation when it comes to the hurt of one of them. The other has no choice but to be drawn into the hurt or difficulty, maybe in a different manner or degree, but they are still influenced by the circumstance. Their life will also be altered to accommodate changes, simply because they are married and share time space and resources. Sometimes the hurt can involve both of them equally.

When a hurt includes a married couple they probably have different viewpoints on how to handle it, again simply because males and females think differently as previously stated. Although easier said than done, each needs to try understanding how the other is thinking, feeling, and desires to deal with the difficult situation or hurt. The outcome has a bearing on them both and not necessarily the same way. Communication is the key. Most people are not mind readers, so talk to each other! Remember marriage takes two, you are not the only one involved. God gave you a mate to help share responsibility and burdens. Be honest, forgiving if needed, and compromise in love for the benefit of the marriage and each other.

Other ways a hurt can directly affect you is because of family. Depending on the closeness of the relationship, like a child or parent, brother or sister, as to what involvement you personally have. It could even be someone outside the family that you depend on or have a personal relationship with.

We are all connected to someone somewhere and for good reasons. Strength, support, encouragement, or the assistance needed when ones personal ability is lacking.

HOW THE HURTING FEEL

People are curious and seem quickly drawn to the troubles of others. That's why the nightly news and some reality shows are major parts of all the television networks. It's usually the negative or bad things that have the biggest crowd of observers. We are all curious about some new development or change from the normal routines, especially in the lives of those we know, and we usually have an opinion as to how it should be handled.

Although we are compelled to find entertainment in the miseries of others, compassion is another human trait God installed in us. We usually root for the underdog, and wish for the right thing to be done with the best possible outcome.

In the beginning of a difficult situation or hurt, friends and relatives are willing to give advice and are right beside you to help. However, after time when things don't seem to be working out or changing for the better they have a tendency to back off. Possibility thinking they can't really help, or feel they may make the situation worse and be blamed for it. They may also get tired of it, besides they have lives of their own to live, it's not really their problem.

For those who wish to come along side, let me tell you how the hurting person feels:

Below are seventeen descriptive words with a short explanation as to how or what the hurting may or already are experiencing. The list I'm sure doesn't hit everything, but what is here can give the helper/support person some insight, as well as reveal to the hurting person they are not alone, and others do understand their pain.

These descriptive words do not fit every situation or type of hurt. They can also come at different times during the healing process and sometimes long after.

Please read these with an open mind, think on them, don't try to justify or blow them off as if they mean nothing, let the words and their explanations penetrate. If nothing else, think of your own life and how these descriptive words of emotion have influenced the difficulties you have experienced, and how you may have dealt with them.

- Exposed - Placed on a pedestal for all to observe, instead of hidden in the normal routines of life. They think and feel they are on public display, and everybody is talking about them.

- Vulnerable - They feel weak, believing others will take advantage of them in their weakened condition.

- Fearful - Experiencing the unknown is scary, it is intimating to deal with things someone is not accustomed to. One particular fear, is making wrong decisions that could result in losing ground.

- Inadequate - Inexperience in a particular circumstance. They are asking how can I do this? I can't handle what is happening. I'm not smart enough, strong enough, or I lack the necessary abilities and resources.

- Robbed - Time has been taken from them. They are at the mercy of others who make decisions for them. They are unproductive and set aside for as long as this issue dominates their life.

- Humiliated – Their reputation is tarnished or ruined, Their place in society has changed. They feel they have lost the respect and favor of others. Whatever dignity they had possessed is lessened or eliminated.

- Valueless - To society, family, and socially, simply because they are no longer involved or complete. They feel unproductive, pushed aside. Self worth is all but gone.

- Selfish - The spotlight is on them because things are not the norm. They have lost control and feel guilty for being the center of attention.

- Despair - Life's plans and goals have been changed without their consent or input. Hopes and dreams have been put on hold or from their viewpoint, completely dashed. There is nothing to look forward to.

- Tired - Struggles in life wear us out. It's harder to keep up when we need to deal with additional issues in life. It can be even more tiring, with time and severity.

- Judged - They self judge, feeling they must have done something to deserve what they are enduring. They also feel those who know them are forming opinions as to why they are going through this.

- Frustrated - This is not the way they wanted it or planned it, and they can't seem to fit in. Whatever they have tried or are trying, does not bring the desired conclusion or change.

- Confused - Not sure what they should be doing, what the solution is, they are lost for direction. They are overwhelmed as they try to deal with many new and unknown things.

- Stagnant - Life is stuck and they can't seem to get it moving. They feel left behind and wish for life to get back to a normal routine of usefulness.

- Stressed - Trying to accomplish or deal with things beyond the norm adds strain to life, usually due to lack of time or resources. Too many things to deal with at the same time, overwhelms and frustrates.

- Dependent - The option to be independent and self-sufficient has been ripped away. They know they need help, but hate the intimidation and humility that come with it. They feel like a burden on family and friends. Its possible they may become recluse and withdrawn, trying desperately to hold their own.

- Lonely - Others withdraw to give them space, or don't want to adjust their own routines to fit the now changed lifestyle of the hurting. They feel set aside from the usual communication, activities and friendships.

- Alone – How could someone else possibly understand, unless they went through the same type of difficulty? Change of lifestyle and emotional stress disrupts relationships.

They want to give up, because they are just worn out, tired, confused and uncertain what the future holds for them. They feel condemned, judged, second-class, and sometimes even get the feeling of being tolerated by those who once seemed to care. Things will never be the way they were, personal lifestyle changes are forced upon them without their consent or choice. The new normal will take time to make necessary adjustments. Changes can be difficult to accept or implement. The lifestyle and comfort zone one had enjoyed are suddenly and abruptly altered, forcing them to make adjustments they didn't necessarily want, and certainly didn't think they would ever need to make.

If they could escape from the present predicament, go back in time, or hide from all the negative issues bombarding them, most normal people would not hesitate to take one of those options. However those options are usually not available, so we grudgingly face what we must.

If someone is willing to come along side, the burden shared is easier to bear. We all need encouragement sometime during life. Encouragement can be as simple as knowing someone cares. A listening ear, a smile, a hug, or even time spent. These things don't really cost the giver much, possibility some time along with a willing and compassionate heart.

One of the unspoken fears the hurting deal with, is how others view them now. Its probable with whatever life has dealt you, your status has changed. It may be a divorce, a child, some other relationship, the death of someone close, even a job change, all of which can immediately alter your social status.

Another hurt with dramatic results can be a financial decay, which can quickly ostracize you from the lifestyle and friends that you had been involved with and enjoyed. There could be an accident sickness or disease, causing limitations on your body and abilities.

It is not necessarily that those around or involved in our lives ceased to care. So please don't make a quick decision to judge them as you wish them not to judge you.

A few things happen during these transitions we need to observe. First if someone has not been where you are, it is next to impossible for them to totally understand. They may hold back fearful of the situation, just like you they also fear the unknown. Next the hurting individual needs to understand it is their life that is changing, not someone else's. This is hard to swallow, as we are quick to compare and rationalize the picture from where we are. We may even secretly wish our difficulty on someone else, because we feel they deserve it more than we do. It is only a normal human reaction, to process in our minds all the reasons we don't deserve what has transpired.

Let me be frank, although this is hard to address I feel it really needs to be stated. When a persons life gets to the point of despair, when they see nothing left for them to look forward to except misery, suicide will cross their mind. It happens, we can't just sweep it under the rug or ignore it, it happens. I didn't say they considered it, I said it crossed their mind. It's because they are thinking of all the possibilities to change their present situation. We make choices everyday and it is the choices we make that define who we are. Hopefully when someone thinks of the extreme choice of suicide, they quickly dismiss it and choose life, realizing there are hope, help, and love that can pull them through their time of bleak despair.

I need to point out to both the hurting and the helper, we do not get to choose what type or the degree of difficulty a trial in life brings us. Our human logic wants to analyze all such encounters with a conclusion of who is to blame, always asking the "why" question. We will discuss that issue in the next chapter.

It does not take many years of living in this uncertain world, to draw the conclusion that it is much easier to look back to understand why things worked the way they did in our lives. Fortunately we cannot see ahead, if we saw how much difficulty we might possibility be destined for, it might drive us to the grave prematurely. Having the present to deal with is probably pushing our limits already. God is merciful by allowing portions (and hopefully some relief between times of trouble) instead of everything at once.

I Corinthians 10:13 states: "No temptation has seized you except what is common to man. God is faithful, he will not let you be tempted beyond what you can bear. But when you are tempted, he will also provide a way out so that you can stand up under it."

It's not unusual to interpret temptation to mean our trials or difficulties. Just reading or hearing that verse, makes most hurting people want to scream! They feel they have personally had to endure more than they can handle. They want relief or an answer now, the pressure is too great, they feel that all viable options have faded away and greatly desire to hide from life until things turn around.

Actually, this is a verse of encouragement! It reminds us we are not the first person who has ever endured something, and that God is there for us if we allow him to be. We can and will get through whatever our disruption is, with his help. Psalms 33:4 "For the word of the Lord is right and true, he is faithful in all he does". In a world full of trouble and uncertainty, there is comfort knowing that he is faithful. We can actually count on things being exactly like his word says, unlike the every man for himself world we presently call home.

Another factor that plays a huge role in a hurting situation causing much anguish and discomfort, is guilt. Guilt is a feeling of personal responsibility, blame or accountability for how something has turned out. It is hard to portray in words how guilt influences our decisions. The guilt factor can be on both sides, from the hurting to the helper and for different reasons. The hurting feels guilt for receiving undeserved attention and gifts. The helper may feel guilty for not being able to find the right words, not being able to be there at the appropriate time, or having the necessary resources to give relief to someone in need. Both sides need to have the emotional flexibility and understanding, to allow the other to be what they can, when they can. It simply boils down to, don't judge others and do the best you can with what you have. We have a tendency to judge things we do not understand, while shying away from things we feel we can't control.

Decisions are made with the information we have, and more times than not, we lack enough information to make a qualified decision, especially pertaining to other people's circumstance or situation. Is it that hard to give others the benefit of doubt, or to love them unconditionally as Christ does us?

One critically important note I need to make to those whose friends or family are dealing with hurt, or life changing situations. If you are the person God wants you to be, the following four-word statement should penetrate deeply. You will also change, its inevitable, let me explain. Just by continuing the relationship you have with the hurting individual, you soon realize that your role as a participant has to change. The relationship cannot remain the same simply because things are not the way they used to be. Therefore, you need to make adjustments in your own life, to accommodate the changes in your friend or relative's life.

If you desire to help yourself or others during trying times, you need to know how emotions and attitudes can, and do play into relationships. Life is made up of personal choices and relationships. God made us to be relational not lone rangers, we need each other and we also need God, who just happens to be our ultimate source for everything.

Relationships take communication, and consideration. The first thing required of you, is the willingness to allow someone into your life at an intimate level. Helping or being helped is shared responsibility that can only happen, if both sides trust each other and have the same goal. This principle is applicable not only for human interaction, but also with God in our personal or spiritual lives.

Let me put it another way. It takes the right person at the right time, with the right attitude for the right purpose. Proverbs 17:17 says "A friend loves at all times". We have all heard of fair weather friends. You know when someone's social class changes or maybe they have a slightly different opinion. Maybe something better comes along, or you get involved you may need to change. A friend loves at ALL times, love is a commitment. My dictionary tells me commitment is responsibility. Put yourself aside and take on the role regardless of your personal opinions. Remember, relationships take work or effort, including proper communication and consideration, only when we grasp and embrace this reality, can we properly share whatever the burden is.

Don't think of getting involved as a one sided event. Yes, you may be the one doing all the receiving or all the giving at this present time. However, as believers we serve a God who rewards and gives blessing to those who do things with the right motivation and attitude. Consider the possibility of gaining a deeper relationship with others, as well as growing in the knowledge and understanding of who you are as a child of the king. Don't do something out of duty or obligation, but with a willing spirit done unto God.

So when something alters your lifestyle in a manner you do not prefer or did not plan for, where do you turn? Who do you go to for advice, support, or help? It is only practical we seek someone or something that has the ability to help us, a greater power than ourselves. For a child it might be the parents, for an employee a boss. If you got hurt physically it only makes sense to see a doctor, or spiritual issues to seek help from a spiritual leader. Even when your pets are in need of something, they come to you with anticipation of your being able to supply them with whatever they have need of.

WHY ME, WHY NOT?

Time to switch gears. So far it seems everything has had some kind of negative overture. I do not wish to dwell on the negative, but also not to ignore what is part of the world in which we live. Let us take a look from a different perspective. Yes, there are positive things to talk about even when it seems your world has turned upside down.

Did it ever occur to you that the situation God has allowed in your like is for the benefit of others? Maybe it's not even about you. Maybe God has given you the privilege and responsibility of being used for his purpose. We do not always see the whole picture or understand the whole issue, that's why Christ talked about living by faith so much. Don't think for even a split second that God doesn't know what is happening in your life.

Psalms 139:2-4 "You know when I sit down and when I rise. You perceive my thoughts from afar. You discern my going out and my lying down. You are familiar with all my ways. Before a word is on my tongue you know it completely, O Lord". Psalms 139:16 "All the days ordained for me were written in your book before one of them came to be". Matthew 10:30 "Even the very hairs of your head, are all numbered."

Whatever has come into your life, God knows about it. He knows every little detail about you right down to how and what you think. It is no mistake that God has chosen you for the circumstance you are now dealing with. We don't receive blessings without having a reason to receive them. Trials birth opportunity for us to make choices, and blessings are a direct result of making right choices. It is even possible you are blessed to be a blessing to someone else!

Somehow we perceive ourselves different than those around us. It can't happen to me, because I have lived right or have taken every possible precaution to prevent whatever from happening. It doesn't always work that way. Nobody is exempt from having negative issues infiltrate their lives at some time. It will happen, and how we deal with it is what really matters!

In the prior chapters we discussed what hurt is. Doing an about face, lets explore the opposite. Think about what life can be if no obstacles sidetracked you, how you want to live, what goals ambitions or things you desire to achieve. Who do you desire to become or what could you possibility be remembered for?

Just changing our thought pattern to anticipated and hopeful things, probably brought some kind of excitement, enthusiasm, and maybe even a smile to your face. If we are completely honest and had everybody and anybody take a survey, I believe the answers would be exactly the same. We all desire contentment, joy, peace, fair treatment, stability, friendship, to be needed and loved, while having our basic needs met.

Let me suggest a few things to broaden your thinking, possibly changing for the positive any perspective you presently embrace concerning what life may have tossed your way.

1. Let God use you. As hard as it is to be humbled into needing someone to come along side in times of despair, God wants us to allow him to supply through others such as: Accepting gifts, with the mindset that all things come from God, so we should thank him accordingly. Even asking him to bless those who have helped you (whether it be emotionally, financially, physically, or spiritually). Remember to keep things as private and personal as possible, because God rewards those who do things in secret, and we certainly don't want others to lose their reward or blessing, because we exploit their choice to honor God by helping others. I'm not saying don't thank the helper, I'm only suggesting you don't make it a public show. If you are the giver, sometimes being anonymous makes it easier for both sides.

2. Maybe God is using you as the needy person, to allow someone else to be tested or used by God for his glory. Graciously let them help without trying to analyze why they are coming along side. Whatever reason they have for supporting you is between them and God. Your position of gratitude should not just be to the person of support, but also to God the ultimate provider. It is a privilege to serve God, and sometimes serving is being the one who needs help.

3. Encourage others. Being a needy person can and usually is very humiliating and sometimes intimidating, but we need to learn how to accept the position given us. Did it ever occur (as the needy person) YOU can be the encourager and be blessed for it? Somebody is always watching you, trying to evaluate what type of relationship you have with God and man. Maybe they can see who God is by watching you under pressure. Consequently they will either be encouraged, or discouraged by the way you handle the trial. You may wish to disagree with that statement, but if honest I believe you actually watch others when they endure hardships too. Probably drawing some kind of conclusion as to how they let God fit into it. Maybe you are able to endure life's difficulty due to the

faithfulness of a believer who set a good example for you. Let that be an inspiration for you to be faithful through your hurtful or unwanted circumstance.

4. Pray for others taking the focus off self. God told us to love our neighbor. What can be a better way than to lift them up before the heavenly father? Just because you find yourself in an undesirable and uncomfortable environment, does not make you the center of the universe. God is relational, meaning we belong together or we need each other. As believers in Christ we are family, brothers and sisters of equal value through the blood of Christ. Families should care about each other and live in unity. I encourage you to lift your family members up in prayer, and in doing so you actually encourage yourself. When a prayer is answered, the family rejoices and is encouraged just by knowing God hears, answers, and is capable to do the same for each of them. Praying for others shows genuine concern. We can pray anywhere, at anytime, and always have immediate, direct access to God the father through Jesus Christ.

5. It may not even be about you! God tells us he causes the sun to rise on the evil and the good,

he sends rain on the righteous and the unrighteous. Sometimes you are just a victim of a sin filled world. We don't always see the whole picture so we must learn to live by faith, believing God knows best when he allows unexplainable or disappointing things in our lives that may cause us to ask the why question.

6. Stop complaining for what God has allowed. We don't usually get a choice determining the type of trial that has infiltrated our lives, but we do get a choice in our attitude. Our attitude of acceptance or bitterness has a dramatic bearing on the outcome. Who are we trying to please? What do we want for an outcome? Do we place blame, or find excuses for our behavior? Are we looking for the opportunities the trial may allow that would not be there if things were "normal"? Will we miss out on blessings because of our attitude? James tells us in James 1:2 to "Consider it pure joy" when trials come. Most normal reactions to difficulties in life would rarely count it joy, but when we study in depth what results transpire from these undesired situations, it makes sense. Those who have gone through dark and treacherous times, gain wisdom, understanding, and come out strengthened.

7. Training is pushing one self beyond normal routines. You may feel its school of hard knocks, but think of it as training to be a leader. Maybe the training is to help you understand and relate to others who may soon be dealing with the same type of circumstance, thus building a relationship that certainly would not have been possible otherwise. Could it be this trial is to build your faith and endurance for some bigger responsibility God has destined you for in the future?

   Strength comes from adversity, we learn much quicker from experience than any other way. All the things that are overwhelming you at the present time are nothing less than birth pains. We all know most women would rather not endure the pains before the birth of their child, however without them new life cannot happen. Is it possible the trial or situation you are presently enduring, is nothing less than "birth pains" for the new life God has for you?

8. Change the WHY to, now what? Look ahead and determine where this particular situation will take you. What possibility does this open for you that may not have been possible if it didn't exist? We all know it is very unusual

for problems to just dissolve or work themselves out. We need to come to the undeniable conclusion that it does exist, we are involved, and for us to sit back and have a pity party benefits nobody. Think through the issue at hand and start making necessary changes to deal with what has transpired.

One of my favorite movies is the Christmas classic "It's a wonderful life". George Bailey the main character seems stuck in a small town, always just scraping by taking responsibility and risk without reward for the benefit of others who are in need. The movie tells the story of how George had touched and influenced many people during his life, even though he felt like he only just existed. He watched friends and family excel, some in position while others grew in wealth, meanwhile he was stuck living in a rundown house, never able to find the time or resources to leave the town he had come to regret. When his world fell apart due to things beyond his control, he saw no reason to continue living and wanted to give up. He even went as far as to say he wished he had never existed.

Sound familiar? It shows how we compare ourselves to others, how we feel we fit in, or our desire to be treated in a fair manner. The picture applies to all aspects of our lives (physical, financial, emotional, and spiritual). We just want to give up, or quit when things don't go the way we expect or desire. We have convinced ourselves that whatever effort we have put into something has not paid off, thus it was not worth our time or effort. To continue would only add personal costs and disappointments. We get sick of giving without receiving, we expect to be rewarded for our time and to be treated fairly. When we feel slighted, our first instinct is to ask the selfish question, what about me?

Two things I want to highlight here, the first is for you to think about how you affect others. What influence or impact your life has on theirs. I'm not just talking physical, I want to emphasize the emotional and spiritual as the two biggest and most important ways we connect to others. It's about relationships, a bond or connection.

Relationships matter, I cannot stress the importance of how we need relationships with other people. Relationships take communication from both parties. Please don't skim over this, slow down enough to grasp the importance of that statement. Communication is a connection or understanding with someone else.

One disclaimer I need to clarify. Communication with someone does not constitute a relationship. A relationship takes commitment, understanding, and involvement!

Let your mind recall some of the ways you have been an impact on others, whether for the good or bad. Then think about how others have impacted you. Stop reading for just a few seconds and really think about the how and why these people have influenced you.

Hopefully those who have impacted you, have done so for positive outcomes and growth in your life. If the impact was negative, it could bring bitterness or separation of relationships. That's not the way God designed us or intended for us to love and care for one another.

May whatever practical applications you have learned from your own lifes experiences, cause you to influence others only in ways that may enhance their relationships with God and man. Positive things have a tendency to reinforce or encourage, isn't that what we should be aiming for?

The second thing I want to inform you of: (Back to the movie "It's a wonderful life"), is the outcome of Georges life. His world came crashing down and he saw nothing positive to look forward to. He was then given the rare opportunity to see how the world may have been if he had not existed. He slowly began to grasp the reality of how he had helped others during their time of need. He saw how he had influenced a whole town for good. In his own time of need they were there for him, the people loved and supported him because of who he was. It was only then, that he understood his purpose in life and gladly accepted it.

Although George was not well off financially, the people called him the richest man in town. It was because of the relationships he had with them, a connection by giving of self. Shouldn't that be the goal of all mankind? Can you imagine how the world might change for the better if we all lived with that philosophy?

If I could somehow imbed something deep in your conscience, it would be to remember you are not an island. Life can and will unexpectedly change, there are no guarantees other than God. Every person is valuable, we are all one of a kind creations made by God himself. Don't ever think or let someone else persuade you that your life doesn't matter, it does!

When our comfortable world of routines and safety zones suddenly and unexpectedly change, we often find ourselves thrown into situations of uncertainty and confusion. It is common to experience things previously unknown and often scary, not to mention the self-judging that so often accompanies such disorders. We hate the thought of having to depend on someone else for support. At these times in life we feel venerable because of having to make decisions we never expected to make.

1 Corinthians 14:33 says "For God is not a God of disorder but of peace". Satan wants us to be confused, discouraged and defeated. Don't let him have that pleasure, seek God and the peace that only he can give, remember he cares for every individual, that includes you!

God desires a relationship with each of us, he is committed, understands, and wants to get involved. He is ready willing and able. As I stated previously, relationships take commitment and involvement on both sides. We humans are ultimately the ones who choose to complete the spiritual relationship, by getting involved through prayer and the reading or studying of Gods word.

Sometime in life and for some, multiple times, we have no choice but to rely on the help of others. Treat others as you desire to be treated. Come gently along side as a helper, or humble yourself enough to let others in when you need them. Its tough on both sides because we want to be an island, we don't want to get involved because it might cost us personally, or worse it might affect who we are. We all know how to "Do the right thing". So what is it that gets in the way? I suggest pride and or selfishness.

Bankrupt, is a nasty word that has weighed heavy on my mind due to what life had brought me personally. Maybe your situation isn't financial, but that doesn't mean you haven't experienced bankruptcy of another kind. A friend of mine who is suffering with a disease that limits his physical abilities, told me he felt bankrupt. The term simply meant to him, that the life he had known before the diagnoses, came to a screeching halt. He had no choice but to make drastic changes or adjustments to accommodate what was taking place. He, like so many others had come to a point of reevaluating life due to circumstances. Learning to live life with a new set of rules.

Although it is hard to stop dwelling on what we lost, even when we know it was beyond our control, we really have very little choice but to persevere, continue, go on, or try our best with what resources and abilities allow. Always remember how you influence or affect those around you! That should be the priority, that's what matters!

So again why you? Let me ask you one more pointed question, who is better off in the end? I suggest it is the person who has been faced with circumstance that pushed them into growth. It's easy to be lazy and comfortable and most of us would rather choose the easy way. I know I would, how's that for honesty? When we lose things we took for granted, or are forced to look beyond ourselves by needing others, we have opportunity to grow, become thankful, and somehow obtain a better understanding of why we exist. So why not you?

MERE WORDS

First impressions last. Have you ever noticed how quickly we categorize someone due to their speech? We judge them by the type of words they use, and the tone of voice in which they express them. We may not even see the individual talking, but quickly make a mental picture as to what type of person they probably are.

If the words and portrayal of them are the same type we use, there seems to be an instant bond because we feel they are somehow like us. If the words are soothing, comforting, positive, energetic or interesting, we may desire to meet that person, with the possibly of getting to know them because of their charisma. If we are offended, put down or challenged by someone's words, we tend to steer clear, not wanting them to influence us in like manner or allow ourselves to be brought to their level.

Can you see where I'm going with this? Our words can quickly make or break a relationship, and it's really hard to get a second chance. First impressions last and it is very easy to ruin a reputation or lose respect. I need to caution you that it is not only the words themselves that matter, but also how they are portrayed, presented and perceived.

What is your intent or motive when approaching someone? It shouldn't matter whether you are the one hurting or the one who is trying to help the hurting. Both sides need to realize and understand, that once something is said especially in the wrong way, it can't be easily taken back. People are fickle, they don't forget and second chances are hard to get. The very thing you desired to do like encourage or find a common bond to build a relationship, instead may have offended and discouraged both of the parties involved.

The best insight I can give for a picture of in depth understanding is to place yourself in the other persons shoes, try to see things from their point of view. This may help you relate and be sensitive not only to their situation, but their emotional and spiritual needs as well.

One aspect we tend to overlook on a personal basis is hearing ourselves speak. Our ears hear what comes out of our own mouths. We all know that if we hear something enough times, we tend to start believing it. Sometimes things are said simply because we previously heard something similar somewhere, and although we have not really thought it through ourselves, or checked to see if it was solid information, we repeat it as if it were fact.

When a thought comes to mind and seems to fit, we portray the words as if we have great insight. We have not only lead whoever we are speaking to into believing that our words of advice are correct, but as we hear the words ourselves actually confirm in our mind, our belief that we have said is true. So not only are we possibly misleading others and abusing trust, but we may also be ignorantly misleading and deceiving ourselves. The message should be clear, make sure what you are saying is true and appropriate. Caution, be sure brain is engaged before putting mouth in gear!

James 3:8 says "But no man came tame the tongue, It is a restless evil, full of deadly poison." Words do matter, they do have affect on others for the positive or the negative, those words spoken to freely have a lasting influence. I strongly urge you to not only to be careful with your speech while trying to comfort or help someone, but listen to what is coming from your mouth. Is it correct and acceptable? Are you willing to take the heat if you misdirected a family member or friend? Is this the kind of help you might appreciate if you were the hurting?

I too am convicted by these same questions, needing to give my thoughts and speech over to prayer daily. Certainly the worst conclusion someone might draw at this point is to just give up and say, I'm not willing to get involved if I might mislead or discourage. That's nonsense and nothing less than an excuse. Take the option of getting involved, but be concerned that yours words are factual instead of just giving your opinion and preferences. Yes mistakes can and will be made, but we learn from our failures and grow. Trying is worth more than failure.

Don't ever believe your words will have no impact! Your words of encouragement regardless of how little you believe they matter, are not wasted. A hurting person has the tendency to hold onto every word, and although they may not express it, really appreciate the effort you have made. They see beyond the words to the attitude, and understanding compassionate heart behind what is being said.

Sometimes our words however innocent intended, can be devastating for those we wish to comfort. A young lady shared with me how when she lost her mother to cancer, those whose intentions were good made comments like: At least she didn't suffer much, or at least you still have your father. She told me those words cut deep, because she felt in a sense they were not allowing her to grieve by trying to minimize the loss she felt.

Another thing I have experienced due to the lack of income causing my own trial, are those who unwittingly (I do not hold that against them) tell me about all the good things going on in their lives. Vacations, retirement, new toys, concerts, going out to eat, and even overtime at their jobs, just to let me know how good things are for them. I can only imagine as some read this, your thinking so what? Why do you even bring these things up?

When things are bad in your life, everything and anything looks better than where you are. Troubles magnify and multiply all the things that have been ripped away from you, including people and the comforts of a normal life.

All these fore mentioned things become hurtles of jealousy, envy, desire, sometimes causing sin. They can be stark reminders of what has been removed, at least temporarily from life. I am not trying to diminish the fact that your life is good, as a matter of fact I truly am happy for you and even pray things may continue to go well. What I am trying to say is that emotions are tender, self worth is being questioned, and personal goals have been put on hold. Anything you say however intended, is perceived as a reminder of what life has become.

For the helper to make conversation with the hurting, showing their genuine interest to be part of their life during difficult times is greatly appreciated. The hurting person sometimes has to deal with personal attitude issues the helper is not aware of. Although no fault of yours, when you speak of how good life is for you at the present time, you sometimes unintentionally put the hurting person in a spiritual battle. Help them win the battle against the sins of envy, jealousy, and possibly bitterness. My only comment or point is for you to be aware of how the hurting person may compare themselves to you, and what emotions it can bring up.

Words matter, I can say it no better or plainer than that. We can build up or tear down in just a few words. Once spoken, words cannot be taken back. We are given two ears to hear and they are always open for business. However we are given only one tongue with two guards, our teeth and our lips. Maybe God gave us more ears than mouth because he wants us to listen more than we speak.

From my own experience and some observation of others dealing with negative circumstances in life, I want to make a pointed comment. If hurting people believe or feel that those around them regardless of their intentions are putting them on the defensive, they will go into seclusion, hide or avoid others simply for self preservation.

If you notice someone withdrawing don't give up, but have the right heart and motive as you continue being an encourager. That doesn't mean hound them, but rethink how you may have incorrectly approached and what may be a better way. An apology may even be necessary to gain back the needed respect for you to be the vessel of encouragement.

A caring person considers the how and what they are presenting with their words and attitude. Proverbs 17:22 "A cheerful heart is good medicine" Proverbs 10:32 "The lips of the righteous know what is fitting" Proverbs 15:1 "A gentle answer turns away wrath".

Words are usually direct from the heart, they are representations of our personal convictions and priorities. We can only be encouragers presenting the right words to those who need them when they need them, if we personally have the right relationships with both God and the one we are coming beside.

I cannot emphasis enough, the importance of how our words directly and immediately affect those around us. May we not only be aware of the words we speak, especially at the critical times of hurt during someone's life, but how we present them. Attitude, tone, timing, and compassion, play major roles and need to be properly spoken, for your words of encouragement to be useful. If presented in a sarcastic, put down, bad timing, or a pull yourself up by the bootstraps attitude, you will lose the opportunity to be of any help to the hurting person. They quickly write you off as someone who is only there to fill some kind of obligation, or self-serving ego trip.

Words are not just words, they have definitions and meanings attached to them. Common knowledge illustrates that some people have the ability to talk a lot and say nothing, while others speak very little but have much to say. One of my favorite sayings is, the more people talk the less others listen. We may laugh at that, but we all know its true and probably can name a few people that either draw our respect or disrespect because of this principle.

Speaking words is only part of the communication or connection we have with each other. When we speak there are signs that are very visible to the other individual, we read past the words to see if the person is genuinely concerned. The tone in which we present ourselves through body language, respect and purpose. These things may be in the form of eye contact, impatience, pity, interest, obligation, support, involvement, depth of conversation, time, and clarity.

Choose your words wisely and present them with a caring heart. Remember the person you are trying to come along side of to help is hurting and needs encouragement more than advice or opinions.

Words are like a pebble thrown into water. There may be a small splash when there is contact, but the ripple can go a long distance, moving or influencing things far from the present situation.

DON'TS

There are times when we wish someone made a list of what to do or say, to bring about the right response in difficult situations. There are certain things we all do or say, maybe even unwittingly that simply irritate a situation instead of helping it. We usually don't realize we are going about it the wrong way, simply because we have not been there and consequently do not understand how it effects the one we are trying to be sympathetic to.

Getting others to understand hurting people is my main goal in the next two chapters as I make a few suggestions from personal observation and experience. Those who are presently hurting will read this and find themselves relating to the different observations. As stated a few chapters earlier, sometimes we need help putting our feeling into words.

Following is a list of thought proving observations that may be helpful in dealing with other people, during times of hurt or difficulties. I have two categories, the Don'ts – what not to do or say, and in the next chapter the Do's, practical ideas of how to come along side someone when their life has been altered without their consent. Seldom is a hurt we may experience expected. Hurts usually come unexpectedly and without respect of who we think we are. The last thing anybody dealing with the negative aspects of life, is for another human to kick them when they're down.

The only disclaimer I place before expressing the Don'ts, is that I know it is impossible to adhere to all of these. However if we are aware of the things to avoid when trying to help others, we can be more effective in our efforts. The motto of a helper should be to help or encourage, not hinder or frustrate.

There will be times during your coming along side someone, words will slip or conversations slide into some gray areas. Don't let that discourage you as the helper. It means more to the afflicted that you are trying, than the possibility of bringing negative results due to a few misplaced words. Effort trumps mistakes every time, the hurting person will overlook mistakes when they understand your heart. Be sensitive enough to say things in a considerate manner.

First the don'ts:

1. Don't judge –

You probably don't know the whole story.

   They may just be a victim of circumstance.

Matt. 7:1-2 Tells us we are judged in the same way we judge others. Do you want that pressure?

2. Don't give advice –

> Giving advice is like kicking them when they're down.

In a sense you are telling them you are smarter than they are, devaluing them.

It's okay to give advice, only if they ask for it.

3. Don't ask them "How are you doing" –

> You may already know the answer, and for them to reply is bringing up negative feelings.

Instead say, Its nice to see you, or I'm glad you're here. I'm happy I can be here with you.

If they really want you to know something, they will tell you. Don't push it.

4. Don't forget or avoid them –

> Loneliness, boredom and low self-esteem are enemies, they need companionship and support.

Usually difficulties last for a period of time, they need you for as long as the trial exists.

Even if the situation has run its course, there may be lasting effects.

It's easier to avoid because you don't know what to do, but they really just need your presence.

5. Don't tell them about all the good stuff in your life –

> This may be exciting for you, but it simply reminds the hurting what life has dwelt them.

Examples: Buying new things, Vacations, Retirement, Job, Bonus, Children, or entertainment.

Understand they are trapped in an environment they can't escape, don't dangle the carrot.

6. Don't join the pity party –

> They really need someone to encourage, not confirm how bad things are.

Smile, listen intently, and allow them to express what they need to.

Tell them you care and value them as a person.

7. Don't talk too much –

> Your presence is more valuable than any words you can muster.

A thoughtless commit like "It can't be that bad" won't win their trust or encourage them.

Talking too much puts the attention on you, making them feel you are there for the wrong reasons.

There are times when they don't want to talk. Nothing personal, just accept and allow it.

8. Don't say let me know what I can do for you -

> The hurting person may not even know what you can do for them.

They feel they are imposing on you by asking for anything, not sure if you meant it.

Just do something appropriate for the circumstance (gift card, meal, money, a night out to listen,

mow the lawn, baby sit, clean their house, fix their car, loan them something, go for a ride together)

Remember it's difficult to accept things that can't be paid back, give without obligation.

Never make them feel they owe you, this adds friction to the relationship and multiplies their pain.

9. Don't start sentences with –

> "At least" or "It could have been worse", "It will get better", or "Your not the only one"

You are trying to minimize the issue, demoralizing them.

In their present condition nothing could be worse.

Allow them the necessary time to work through the emotions that we are created with.

10. Don't ask demanding questions prying for more information, some things need to be kept personal.

> They already feel their life is a public display, allow them some privacy.

Questions frustrate, usually because of the uncertainty, they may not have an answer.

Let them know if they need a listening ear you are available, then make yourself available.

11. Don't say you know how they feel.

> You do not truly understand unless you have been there, only then are you able to relate.

Admit you do not know how they feel, but tell them instead that you feel for them.

12. Don't be the aggressor –

> Let the person you came to encourage, lead or choose the conversation and topics.

If you run the show, it sends a silent message that they are not important to you.

Although these things may sound discouraging to those wishing to come beside, I wish to point out that the feelings and emotions of the hurting are greatly influenced by your approach and especially your words. Starting off on the wrong foot will no doubt be very difficult to fix. The whole reason you came in the first place was to be of help. Therefore come with the right mindset for them, as you would desire they might do for you if the tables were turned.

When hurt happens, in the mind of the one hurting everything is multiplied. Another way of saying it is amplified. The uncertainty, self-worth, doubts, and the perception of what others think. The same goes for the words you speak in a way that may come across negatively. Be careful and considerate, think about how your words may be taken regardless of intent, before uttering whatever comes to mind just to make conversation.

DO'S

I have not been fair with the don'ts, if I leave you hanging with so many negatives. So what CAN you say or talk about? There is no cookie cutter answer to that question, simply because different situations demand different solutions. Again these are suggestions from my personal experiences and observations.

No doubt it is awkward and even invasive to make conversation due to difficult circumstances. It takes a mature person, not only to make the effort but have the attitude of being an encourager or a shoulder to lean on.

The best I can give you for topics of conversation, is to find subjects that are not directly related to the issue or hurt that the person you wish to help is dealing with. Let me remind you as stated in the don'ts chapter, don't be the aggressor, let them lead the topics of conversation if possible.

If money issues, talk about current events, family, sports, bring up past happy memories, or anything that money has no or little relevancy to. Medical or physical, maybe talk about family, pleasant memories, sports, current events. If about the present circumstance let the person involved be the one to bring it up. Emotional and Spiritual can be very touchy and those involved can be anywhere from the one extreme to the other. It is vital we are perceptive to where they are, and especially how they may choose to understand and apply our words of encouragement.

Sometimes its more practical to say as little as possible, being there is more important than any words spoken. If the hurting desires to talk, they will. Your selfless action of being a good listener, shows you actually do care and respect the one you're there for.

Now lets take a look at a few suggestions of what you can do to encourage, with the Dos list.

1. Call, send a card, or stop in –

    Showing you care is encouragement.

    Use discretion per circumstance whether to stop in or not.

    Calling ahead (for home visits) is usually appreciated

2. Listen confidentially without interrupting–

    Sometimes just an expression of feelings to a trusted friend, can be a way of healing.

    Interrupting is telling them you have something more important than what they are saying.

3. Invite them over or take them out for a meal –

    Loneliness and boredom continue to drown them in the thoughts of their difficult situation.

    It might cost you time and money, but treat them as if it were you in their predicament.

    This is an action that shows them you genuinely care, because you are personally involved.

4. Pray for them –

    Pray for Gods will and that they can accept it as such.

    Pray in secret for them, but encourage them by letting them know you are doing so.

    Ask specifically, what you can bring before the Lord on their behalf.

    Continue to pray on their behalf daily, weekly, monthly, or as long as it takes.

    Believe what you pray for can happen.

5. Give them hugs or handshakes –

    Nothing says I care about you like an actual physical touch.

Make it a firm physical touch (if suitable) not some wimpy, I pity you approach.

Even a hand placed on a shoulder or other appropriate location is a way to make it personal.

6. Confirm your interest in them –

    Smile, looking directly in their eyes letting them know its them, you are thinking about.

    Say I care about or love you. A few encouraging words go a loooong way.

7. Allow them to grieve –

    We are made with emotions and need to express them, this is part of the healing process.

    The times of emotional stress is when we make important decisions concerning our maturity.

    Allow them to use you as an unconditional shoulder to lean on.

8. Relief please –

    Discouragement comes when we can't seem to change our environment. Everybody needs a change of pace once in a while, just to renew or refresh the outlook. The difficult issue here is if we have a lack of money, or are physically unable to move into different surroundings, we remain in our familiar stagnant environment, keeping us from being stimulated by outside sources. Try to find a way to change the environment to something positive or different, regardless of how temporary.

To the hurting I bluntly say, you need not feel guilty for it. It is for nothing short of trying to have a better outlook on life, you are trying to get out of the rut of despair. Don't think for a second that because you are in a negative situation, that you need to act like it. Take advantage of opportunities when the door opens!

This suggestion lies heavy on the one who comes beside, for two simple reasons. The one suffering may not be able to implement it, and it's very possible that they may not even be capable at this time to think beyond the present conditions. They really do need your help so don't let them down. Again picture yourself in their place and react accordingly.

9. Make yourself available –

    If you are to busy wrapped up in your own little world, if makes it rather difficult to help others.

    Giving of your time shows the hurting both your humility and their importance.

    Missed opportunities cannot be gotten back when it fits our schedules.

Do's and Don'ts PS

There are other aspects of the Do's and Don'ts that may seem unnecessary to some, but really need to be stated. Again this book is to help those on both sides to be as effective as possible, and not waste good intentions. Giving anonymously is a great way to help and is greatly appreciated. I do wish to address some issues that some may not think about in using this method. Please don't misunderstand my intent to the point of not doing anything, by all means do whatever you feel is right to help those you love when life happens to go sour.

- If you wish to donate (a meal, food items, basic everyday needs, or special gifts) it is helpful to speak to the recipient before doing so. I know this is awkward and if you are not comfortable with the idea it's okay, proceed with your original plan..

- Someone might receive four meals in a row to feed four people when they may be eating alone, and it's possible (hush the thought) they might not like what you took the effort and time to make. One may unknowingly give something full of sugar to a diabetic, or possibly produce an allergic reaction due to an ingredient in the donated dish. Don't misinterpret, the gestures are more appreciated than the gift itself because it shows care and concern. I am only pointing out how at times due to miscommunication, efforts can be misplaced and even misunderstood.
- It is not wrong and they won't be offended, by you asking when or how much, and if there is there something they don't like, or presently need. You place them in an uncomfortable position, if they end up throwing something away for whatever reason, especially when you ask them if they liked it.
- It is very possible when you ask them for the when, or what, they will give a generic answer. Actually you should expect it. Don't give up so easily, again they will not be offended. They are only saying what they are because, first they are not sure if you are serious, and second as a recipient they are humiliated by receiving anything, thus they feel it wrong to make any

request of your generosity. In the end they will be grateful for your insight.
- Number eight on the Don't list was "Don't ask what can I do for you?" Now your asking how to implement what was just stated in conjunction with the last paragraph. Go with a specific item. Let them know you wish to bring a meal then ask for specifics, or if it is a food shower ask for a list of things they could use. Another idea is gifts, maybe their child has a birthday and nobody knows better than the parents what the child might need or desire.
- Generic questions will get generic answers, and it can bring frustration to the hurting instead of helping them. If you genuinely desire to come beside and help, but don't know the how or what, be honest. Tell the hurting you are willing but don't know what to do. Again they will not be offended by your honesty and will probably open up more because of it, and even more so if you have a good relationship with them.
- Gift Cards are a difficult to discuss because nobody in their right mind is going to turn that away. Generally they are a great idea, and a way to say I care while anonymous.
- Gift cards are also always specific. I'm not talking about the dollar amounts, but the

locations of spend ability. They are one hundred percent without a doubt gladly accepted and very useful, simply because the recipient chooses what to spend it on and when to use it. The down side of a gift card is the different spending habits between the donor and the recipient.
- The donor may use a specific store the recipient never goes to or does not have easy access to, particularly distance. The easier you make it for the hurting in times of difficulty the more appreciated it is. The obvious conclusion here is to somehow find out where the hurting person generally shops for their needs.
- There can be a very positive side of the gift card also. Most cards are for gas or food stores, these are for the basics of life. Periodically one may be received for a restaurant, coffee shop, clothing store, or some other beyond the basic everyday needs category. Yes we all need the basics, but the beyond the basics are moral boosters. They can change the environment similar to what was suggested earlier.
- The gift card also has a hidden benefit. It shows the receiver you thought about them, and cared enough to make a special effort by going somewhere to purchase the card. An action that costs time gives

encouragement to the recipient, because of the personal effort it required.

When it comes to money and the management of it for someone dealing with financial difficulties, regardless of how they came to the present condition, we judge. Maybe subconsciously but we still form a personal opinion, grading or categorizing the person or persons involved. When it comes to an accident, sickness, or disease, we generally just accept it because that's the way it is, whoever is involved probably had no choice. With money it's a completely different set of rules.

We believe the persons involved somehow let things slip or evolve into the present condition so it's their own fault. This is entirely possible, however as was previously stated one may have had some physical issue, or accident causing a stress on their personal finances, or they may be a victim of some other circumstance.

Anonymous giving sometimes makes it easier on both parties involved, due to feelings of obligation, motivation, and even possible judging. It also leaves God as the one who gets the credit and praise. My personal opinion is unearned money should always be given anonymously, making God the only choice for praise and thankfulness from the receiver.

Just a note for the sake of information, so this is not one sided. The person receiving the monies is not ignorant of the judging or the way others perceive them in their condition. They are just like you, except that they just happen to be on the other side of the issue at this time in their life. Hopefully with that statement, you now understand why and how the receiver may act or react to their financial needs, and how others influence their decisions.

All that aside, God wants us to love each other unconditionally. Any misuse of funds before it became an issue, and any from the helps that may come as a result of the problem are between God and that person. Both sides need to have the right motivation and be good stewards of what God supplies without judging the other.

Those are a few personal observations to help the hurting and to give the helper insight. If you are one of the hurting, I sincerely hope someone will implement these principles into your life, coming along side for comfort support and encouragement.

If at this time in your own life you are one of the fortunate ones to have things going well, I encourage you to seek out someone less fortunate, then practice these principles. Someday you may be the one needing help or encouragement. It's really not a secret that ultimately, we all depend on someone for something during our lifetime. It may be as simple as a child depending on their parent or perish the thought, a parent that now depends on their child for everyday needs.

You may desire to take some of my observations with a grain of salt, and I accept that. However the issue I will not budge or compromise on is that Gods word is the final authority. I make mistakes but God does not, so I encourage you to seek his will and direction for your life through his word. 2 Timothy 2:15 "Do your best to present yourself to God as one approved, a workman who does not need to be ashamed, and who correctly handles the word of truth."

If I could sum up this section in a few words it would be: Hurting people need to know and experience that someone genuinely cares and is willing to take personal action to show it. Talk is cheap, but time and personal sacrifice speak volumes! Treat others as you wish to be treated.

ADJUSTMENTS

We live in an imperfect world. I hardly need to elaborate on that statement, as everybody reading this will automatically sigh a big don't I know it. The one and only reason we have hurts, problems, difficulties, and other negative things to deal with during our time here on earth, is because of the sin curse!

My personal desire is to encourage and inform all who read this book how valuable they are. You are not alone or set aside by what life brings. You are special and have a purpose for being where you are.

Although we may have a hard time with the concept, here is the honest truth. All of us by nature are sinful, self indulgent, prideful humans. I believe if we can comprehend this concept, we can begin to understand the why, pertaining to the hurts we find ourselves subjected to in life. Not every hurt or difficulty that comes along is because you did something wrong and are being judged or disciplined. Remember the first statement, we live in an imperfect world.

Gods word is absolute and true, it's always relevant and never changes. He talks extensively, of the constant spiritual warfare that is happening on this earth for control of our thoughts, attitudes, motivation, and personal agendas. Below are a few things for each of us to look at in our own lives. Hopefully with wisdom and the right perspective, decisions can and will be made to move beyond your present situation of difficulty.

1. When you are humbled by your circumstances, you learn quickly why not to judge others. Before being there yourself you could not fully understand. To pass judgment, one must know every detail of what may have happened to bring someone else to their life altering circumstance. If you did know and understand, you probably would have an attitude of compassion rather than a judgmental one. An example of this may be of one being childless, only another childless couple can fully relate to the emotions and disappointments involved. God also tells us in Matthew 7:2 "For in the same way you judge others you will be judged, and with the measure you use it will be measured to you". Consider your motivation before passing judgment.

2. Harboring bitterness, envy, or anger, tends to hurt our personal relationships. Rarely does anyone want to hang around a negative person for very long. Seldom does anything good come from hanging onto negative

feelings. These particular types of emotions eat us up from the inside, only hurting ourselves, not the ones who are the subject of our selfish or envious attitude. These things tend to wear us down physically and stress us out emotionally, causing additional problems by placing strain on other areas of our lives.

3. Comparing ourselves to others is actually taking our eyes off God. Nobody wants to hear something so convicting, but truth never changes. We are self-centered by nature and it's a constant spiritual battle for control. God is not a respecter of persons, in other words he doesn't compare you to your neighbor or friends. It does not matter to him what your position is, whom you are related to, how much money you have, or what your status in society is. If we took the challenge of not being a respecter of persons like Christ, we just might live differently. We should not be comparing ourselves to others, but loving and caring for each other as we walk through life together. Don't dwell on comparing yourself to others, it only allows opportunity for dissatisfaction or envy to dominate.

4. The definition of a god is anything that dominates us. God, the real one who created all things seen and unseen, gave us a commandment in Exodus chapter 20 that states: Thou shalt have no other gods before me. So the question is, what is a god to you? What do you pursue? One can tell a persons priorities by the way they spend their time and money. It is not necessarily both time and money, because one may be correctly prioritized while the other selfishly overindulged in. God is very specific with his command when he says "no other god". If we have anything that comes before him, we have in a sense rejected God, or given him at best second place. Anything does not only include things or objects we see, but also things unseen like a friendship, pride in ourselves, a job, or an activity.

5. It doesn't seem like it now but this life is temporary. Therefore it is of utmost importance we keep our eyes on the future, or things we believe are to come (Its called hope). We probably have all heard the expression: Life is like a roll of toilet paper – the closer we get to the end, the faster it goes. That may be somewhat of a funny analogy, but most adults would tend to agree it's more realistic than they care to express.

Again it depends on where you are in relation to something. If we see an airplane in the sky it seems small, but if we are standing right next to it, we wonder how something so big can get off the ground. The big picture is simply that life is short, however when living one day at a time with our limited viewpoint, we have the tendency to relate only to the present situation of what's here and now.

6. You are not the first person to suffer this kind of pain. Throughout history we can find examples of someone who has endured the same or similar, misunderstanding injustice disaster rejection hurts pains loneliness humiliation despair, and other emotions that accompany life's uncomfortable detours. Those areas of negativisms have not changed since the beginning of time, but are prevalent in our present world also.

7. Never give up. I know it's not the first time you have ever heard that. You are probably already on the defensive muttering under your breath, its not quite that easy. I know and understand better than I can express in a few words on a page. Sorrow pain frustration and disappointment are all part of

life, but so are contentment endurance perseverance joy and peace.

Yes, I know the items mentioned above are blunt words. I may even have offended a few people, but I suggest making the necessary adjustments in life. It shows humility character and maturity. The evidence of what we believe to be true comes out in our decisions and actions.

We all have ambitions or goals in life, but the real question for all of us to answer is, what do we want to be remembered for when the temporary journey on this earth is complete? I want to give you three things to ponder.

1. Status – There are many worthy people who hold a position of status, and are used for the progress or benefit of many other people. Status is not wrong if used for the correct reasons. It is actually a responsibility, and should be considered a privilege to influence for the benefit of others. However status can be abused, such as someone who has the wrong attitude by controlling, using, or taking advantage of those under their authority, simply because their abilities or position allow them to.

2. Satisfaction – Another word may be contentment. Again these words and their meanings are not wrong, as a matter of fact they are usually associated with the good or positive things in life. If we are being honest, all of us desire contentment in our lives, it is a major ambition or drive, something we ultimately desire to achieve. The dominant question at this point would be, what is satisfaction? My handy dictionary tells me it is a feeling of pleasure, or happiness when a need or desire is fulfilled. It may be our own needs or even for someone else's that we had the opportunity to be part of. So it all goes back to the why we are in pursuit of something, our motivation, what we expect or feel we deserve, and how to use the resources given us. Those resources may be anything from financial or physical, to comforting words spoken in love for the emotional or spiritual needs of people God has placed in your life.

3. Stuff – Just the word "stuff" generates many thoughts, we all have ideas what stuff is and how it affects us. Material stuff, the things to help us live life, can be used for selfish reasons or to aid us in building relationships. Sometimes the information highway uploads unneeded stuff into our

minds, keeping us from thinking for ourselves. Then there is the stuff of daily living bogging us down, making our lives so complicated or busy we don't have or allow time for God or others. Stuff can be just that, stuff or filler, something to just take up our time and energy while draining us from being productive in constructive ways. Stuff can be prioritized for our own benefit of usefulness as well as those whom we have relationships with.

It does me no good to elaborate further on these issues, I'm sure you have already placed yourself somewhere in the context of these three words and their influences on your personal life. If you have read through these words and mentally thought of how they fit others, I strongly encourage you to reread through them, this time with yourself as the main character.

The me attitude gets in the way of God using us. We all have a tendency to try to hold onto something called control. We hate the idea of losing control because it might force us deal with possible changes in our familiar and comfortable world. Proverbs 3:5-6 says "Trust in the Lord with all your heart and lean not on your own understanding. In all your ways acknowledge him, and he will make your paths straight".

Trust is having confidence in, relying on something or someone to take responsibility for your benefit. Those two verses work together. If we truly trust God (whatever our situation) we want him to direct our paths. Again that can only happen if we have a relationship with him. Psalms 37:23-24 are follow ups that encourage us to pursue Gods way. "If the Lord delights in a mans way, he makes his steps firm: Though he stumbles, he will not fall, for the Lord upholds him with his hand."

I get excited when I read encouraging words like that, just knowing God cares enough to protect me in those times of disillusion and uncertainty, causes me to smile.

If you have accepted Gods word as truth, you know he will never let you down. Adjustments or changes in life are usually hard, and when we fight it alone, it only seems to multiply the frustrations. Accept the changes, give God the burden and allow others to be your support.

Misery loves company – there is more truth in that small phrase than most of us would admit. The real question is why? Probably because it gives comfort to the one in misery, just knowing someone else is feeling the same pain. They find comfort knowing they are not isolated from the rest of society because of their difficulty. Having someone to cry with or relate to in our down times, can ease the feeling of loneliness or confusion that usually come with unexpected detours in life. Companionship, someone to share with or a listening ear, gives comfort and support making things easier.

Jesus tells us he is there as in Matthew 11:28-30: "Come to me all you who are weary and burdened, and I will give you rest. Take my yoke upon you and learn from me, for I am gentle and humble in heart, and you will find rest for your souls. For my yoke is easy and my burden is light." Notice we need to take action and the result should be for us to learn from him, then we will have the desired rest or peace. He does not say the problems will just disappear, but he does promise to be a comfort to us during these times.

What a picture of being there for a brother or sister in time of need. Right beside them taking part of the load, not pushing or pulling like we sometimes tend to do, but right beside sharing the load or burden equally. Anybody that has had help knows the load shared is easier bared.

PERSONAL CONFLICT

Just living on this ball we call earth or home, seems to bring issues of ciaos without explanation, conflict, disagreement, restlessness, and struggles for peace, even when we desire to live a quiet non-conflict lifestyle.

When there is a fight or battle, it's always for the underlying reason of power over, the ability to control, or to have dominance of. This principle is true in both the physical and nonphysical realms. We know from history, that the battles or difficulties in life shape us in multiple ways. We learn from them, are strengthened through them, and hopefully make adjustments because of them.

Living on this earth is the only requirement needed to be a participant in the battle of control. By nature we look out for ourselves, most personal decisions made revolve around where we fit in and how it benefits us.

Just as we change physically when we age, the same should be true emotionally and spiritually. We are not all going to be facing the same trial hurt or uncertainty, but what these difficult times do is the same for all. Life is a journey of growing or maturing, in relationships, faith and hope.

Most of us would rather plead ignorance, desiring to live a peaceful undisturbed life. As much as we wish to avoid conflict, we must acknowledge we are involved in a war! The battle is for control of our minds, will, and the priorities that shape our lives.

I may have lost a few people at this point, so I feel it necessary to elaborate. As I stated previously, the one and only reason we deal with hurts, difficulties, problems, misunderstandings, sorrow, pain, disorder, and negative situations, is because of the sin curse on this earth we live on. Everything in life is subject to this principle, and that is the reason we deal with the struggles we do.

I sincerely hope you do not regard this chapter as being preachy, please hang in there with me. I cannot write what life is about without getting to the basics of what life is. I personally believe we are only on this earth temporarily, but that we live forever. I believe the real reason we are given the opportunity to live on earth is to choose or reject God. Life is about choices of priorities, the difficulties, pain and hurts of living are the tools used to force us into making the decisions that shape our true priorities and convictions.

This battle for the mind is a spiritual one, personally fought by everybody every day. It is a relentless life long struggle of being prepared, being on guard, and engaging the enemy (evil), with outcomes and results that stand for all of eternity.

In the spiritual battle that is taking place in the unseen world all around us, we need not only be aware of who we are, but how we fit in. There is God the heavenly father, Satan the deceiver, and you the one both desire to have allegiance from. God in his wisdom has given each of us, a free will to choose who we will serve and commit ourselves to.

Presently you are asking what this has to do with hurting people, let me explain. Because of the sin filled world in which we live, there is pain, sorrow, tears, and finally death. Those are the results of the sin curse on this earth. Revelation 21:1 tells us, "there will be a new heaven and a new earth, for the first heaven and the first earth shall pass away." Then in verse four it says, "there will be no more death, or mourning, or crying, or pain, for the old order of things has passed away."

Hallelujah, I can't help but get excited. It only stands to reason that if there is no more sorrow, pain, crying, or death, then all our trials, difficulties, and negative circumstances will also come to an end, forever!! That's good news and it gives hope to endure the present situations, knowing God has already won the battle through the sacrifice of Jesus Christ on the cross.

It is hard to look beyond where you are at this very moment, because life still needs to be lived in this present environment. Informed people can make informed choices, so let's look at some of the major facts of what we need to deal with on a daily basis. Then hopefully, we can rise above whatever keeps us from being productive in this life by making wise informed decisions.

As a reminder what we are dealing with, I point out Ephesians 6:12 "For our struggle is not against flesh and blood, but against the rulers, against the authorities, against the powers of this dark world and against the spiritual forces of evil in the heavenly realms". As believers in Christ we are fighting an unseen battle for the mind and the will. The seen things or our physical life on this earth are the battlefield and weapons used to play it out.

Listed below are issues and participants in the spiritual battle we are subjected to daily.

- Who We Are:

A living soul, created to live eternally. A temporary resident on this earth. Made up of a body, mind and soul.

What we should do:

Acknowledge him (God our creator) in all our ways, do all things unto him and not unto man, seek his will. Praise him and thank him. Seek forgiveness from him when we let him down.

- Who God Is:

King of Kings, Savior, Redeemer, Friend of sinners, The I am that I am, The living God that was and is and is to come, Lord, Christ, Messiah, Sovereign, Holy, Just, Father of light, Alpha and Omega, Divine Authority, Judge, Creator of all things, Emanuel, Jehovah, Rabbi, Teacher, Judge, Master, Shepherd, Prince of Peace.

- What he does:

Loves us unconditionally. Provides for our daily needs and protects us. Is preparing a place in eternity for us, controls all things, strengthens us, forgives and forgets our sins if we confess them. Gives grace and mercy. Never changes.

- Who Satan Is:

Deceiver, father of lies, adversary, tempter, serpent, prince of darkness, ruler of this world, accuser of the brethren, author of confusion.

- What he tries to do:

Keeps us so busy we do not have time for a relationship with God. Puts things like: Comparisons doubt fear worry anxiety bitterness envy jealousy loneliness despair, and self-pity in our minds. Tells us to blame someone else or even God when life falls apart. He wants us to fail in our relationship with God. Makes us believe we are self-sufficient. Tells us that sin is fun, but fails to let us know the consequences.

Jesus paid our sin debt on the cross, already defeating Satan. Consequently his alternative plan is to cause as much damage as possible to Gods creation. He wants to destroy you because if he can't do anything to God, he wants to destroy the one thing that has the most value to God, you!

The list above gives a brief overview of who and what God and Satan are. The way they think and act out their character is completely opposite of the other. God, is truth and peace, Satan, is lies and ciaos.

The first thing we tend to do when things don't go as we had hoped or expected, and certainly when the bottom falls out on our lives, is to blame God. We need to start thinking in another direction because the best thing we could do for ourselves is, run to God not from him. He is the only one who genuinely cares about us, with the ability and resources to actually do something.

We need to have the right mindset by submitting to the understanding that everything is done according to Gods will and for his glory, accepting that what he has decided is best for us.

So what happens when we indulge in comparisons, selfishness, or wrong attitudes? Is that the way to escape our troubles, change our circumstances or fix the problem?

The truth is, we all like a pity party once in a while and I'll be the first to admit it. Somehow we justify self-pity by telling ourselves we are comfortable just staying down instead of trying to get back up. Everybody knows it's a lot easier falling down than it is getting up, especially when you keep getting hit over and over again. Sometimes we just want to be left alone, crawl someplace where nobody can find us. A place to hide from trouble where we can feel comfortable, in control, without being made to feel guilty or judged by our peers.

Life is challenging enough when things are normal, if there is such a thing. Often we find ourselves doing what we don't want to do, being where we don't want to be, or dealing with circumstances we would rather have never been involved with. In doing so, even if it was completely beyond our control in the first place, we tend to blame ourselves and even resort to self-pity. Its easy to ask why me, and maybe even easier to come up with many reasons to justify the why not.

More times than not we pray and pray and pray about something, but grow weary and are disappointed when nothing happens in a timely manner. We have all heard the religious biblical answer to this dilemma, God answers in three ways, yes no or wait. Sometimes it's rather difficult to understand or even believe God has a plan and what we are enduring is part of it. We have our own plans or ideas of not only how things should progress, but the timing in which it happens.

Take a step back by remembering two things, one is that all things work for the glory of God. The other is our timing is not always Gods timing. I wish to highlight what happened in Daniels life when he prayed, why his prayer was heard and even how timing was an issue. Read the two verses below and place yourself, and your situation into the scenario. In the spiritual battle we need to have the right relationship and motivation for the right outcome.

Daniel 10:12-13 "Do not be afraid Daniel. Since the first day that you set your mind to gain understanding and to humble yourself before God, your words were heard, and I have come in response to them. But the prince of the Persian kingdom resisted me twenty-one days. Then Michael, one of the chief princes came to help me because I was detained".

The word battle indicates many participates, but at times it feels you are the only one wrestling with the choices that need to be made during unwanted circumstances. Keep your focus correct, look beyond yourself.

Self-pity is not a good character builder. Take the emphasis off the negative and place it on the positive, be thankful. When life bottoms out, the farthest thing from our minds is being thankful. God reveals and encourages us in James 1:2, "Consider it pure joy when you face trials." Joy means happiness or pleasure. It's not the trial we want or desire, but the result of the trial. James finishes by telling us the eventual reward is maturity. I can't imagine anybody who is normal, wanting to be treated as a child their entire life, but rather wanting to fit into society and able to experience the benefits and privileges of being an adult.

Being thankful is an expression of gratitude or appreciation for something done on our behalf. The expression can be in the form of acknowledgement for something, or an unselfish act someone did on our behalf. One way we express ourselves is to verbally speak our thanks. Another way is to give something of ourselves, showing our approval for the act of kindness someone has bestowed upon us. An attitude of gratitude is a solid step in the right direction. Thankfulness is usually a character trait of who we are. Thankfulness is something we don't create for ourselves but is an expression from us for something received from another source.

Thankfulness takes the spotlight off us, and gives meaning to life due to an outside influence. It is impossible to be thankful without thinking of who is responsible for our thankfulness. A pleasant memory can cause a smile due to joy the thing or person we are thankful for brings to our attention. Possibility a sunny day, children, grandchildren, a kind word, a card or time with friends, smells, sounds, the list is inexhaustible.

If we actually took the time to concentrate on just the things we take for granted each day, we might be humbly surprised. We don't appreciate some things until they are taken away. Be thankful for what you have now, thankfulness is a positive emotion that encourages and changes perspective.

I get excited when I think of things to be thankful for. I'm going to bring a few more things to your attention just to get you thinking how we forget and take things for granted. God gave us five senses to use and they each bring us pleasure in different ways. The eyes help us navigate when walking, they allow us to see Gods creation and guide us in many aspects of life. Our noses allow us to identify smells, keeping us from danger as well as giving pleasure. The ability to touch and feel things, aids us in ways beyond the actual touch. Hearing is communication and understanding of whatever or whoever is near us, sounds can give warning or direction. Speaking is also communication, especially the connection with another person, and singing can be part of the speech sense. So often we forget the benefits of music, and the joy or comfort it brings regardless of where we are in life.

All of these senses can bring pain and pleasure or give us information to make decisions that directly effect who we are. These God given abilities also involve emotions and help us relate to those around us. Those are just five things we can be thankful for in life, and there are so many more.

Being thankful is only one way to open a door to the positive, bringing self instigated encouragement. I suggest another challenge for positive reinforcement, pray for other people. Yes, you are going through maybe some of the toughest things no human should have to endure. Look beyond yourself for just a moment and maybe just maybe, someone else is going through something of equal difficulty, and needs your prayers or encouragement.

Prayer not only brings someone else's name and circumstance before our creator, but puts you in Gods presence at the same time. A truly thankful person is a giving person. I'm not necessarily talking about money, I'm referring to self or personal involvement. That may even involve thinking about or putting someone else's problems before your own. Thankfulness can only come from the heart, more than likely that heart has grown to understand what being thankful is because of those trying times in life. Nobody relates to someone suffering like another who is, or has gone through something similar.

So when fighting the daily battle of the will, remember who you are and that the decisions today stand for all of eternity. Don't forget to spend time daily in Gods word and in prayer, so you are equipped to fight the battles of life that you are subjected to every day.

Do your research, know the enemy, ask for help, do what you know is right, don't dwell on the negative, fight with confidence because of who you are!

PERSPECTIVE

How we view things in life is called perspective. We need to take a look at and discuss perspective, because it has more influence than any of us care to admit.

Perspective is a measured assessment of a situation. Measured assessment broken down translates to a comparison. The first place any human naturally goes when comparing is to another human, evaluating what the differences are between them. Basically we come to one of three conclusions:

1. I am better
2. We are similar or the same
3. They are better

These conclusions can be drawn to either people involved, or to lifes circumstances. I do not wish to dwell on the people comparison, other than to conclude that if we are mature in our spiritual life, numbers one and three simply should not exist.

When we compare ourselves with others, we can always find someone to fit the particular criteria we desire. We make ourselves believe we are better or worse than they are, to achieve the outcome we subconsciously have predetermined. So lets look at how these stack up in lifes circumstances.

As previously mentioned we will all go through some kind of trial, or unpleasant time during our lifetime. We may not all go through the same type or degree of difficulty, or even the same number of trying times. These times are what make us who we are, not only giving the influences or criteria that force us to make choices, but refines and defines us by those choices.

Perspective or comparison can be either dangerous or a commendable thing, depending on what we are comparing to and the reasons we draw a conclusion. Drawing conclusions for the right reasons, helps us make wise and useful decisions pertaining to handling of whatever the particular situation is. It's easy to use a comparison to achieve any self-motivated results, which is what our human tendency wants to do. We choose something or someone that elevates us, or puts us in a better light. However, in doing so we have only lied to ourselves and will never be able to make the necessary adjustments to overcome, simply because we have not convinced ourselves we need to change or adapt.

The opposite can also be true. We pick a comparison that looks better than us or where we are, lowering our self worth or self esteem, believing that it's not worth the energy it might take to improve, or possibly being convinced we have no hope of change. Again, we have only mislead ourselves with this kind of mentality.

The next question is hanging heavy. Do we always need to change? Let me rephrase it so the question is aimed directly at each one of us. Are you comfortable in times of difficulty? Are you satisfied with where you are and willing to accept what your life has become? Hopefully you have answered both questions in your mind before you read the conclusion that I have drawn from my own struggles. I perceive you are not comfortable, so yes you do need to change. The reason change is required regardless of where you are, is because life is a process of growing or maturing.

Society moves forward and develops new things that help us meet our daily needs. We have gone from outhouses to indoor plumbing, horse and buggy to cars, and from writing everything on paper to using computers. Just like society changing to benefit mankind, we also need to continue making adjustments in our personal lives to mature. Not too many people want to go back to the old ways, we should think of our personal life in the same sense when it comes to relationships and personal growth.

Then you may ask, does anyone ever mature to the point of being comfortable in lifes uncontrollable situations? Again I remind you, life is a process of maturing that ends only in death. So even if it does get easier to handle things with maturity, we still feel sorrow, disappointment, pain, and the other negative aspects of life in this sin filled environment.

Lets get back to the idea of perspective or comparison. What should we be comparing our lives and its circumstances to? Should it be to other people? No, simply because people change. At times you may be looking good because of somebody and yet at some other point in life, you may not measure up to the same person.

God is the standard, the only one we can depend on as the perfect example through Jesus Christ. He never changes and I'm so thankful he doesn't, otherwise where is our hope? With Christ as our example of comparison, we get a glimpse of our shortcomings and begin to understand why it's an ongoing endeavor.

An example to help understand comparison or perspective, is to revert back to your childhood. Remember the yard or playground where you used to play when growing up? It seemed big enough at the time because of your size, and it was all you really knew. Now when you visit the same yard or playground as an adult, it probably seems small in comparison to how you remembered it as a child. That's because you are bigger now, its not that the play area had become smaller but the fact that you have grown.

Another example from our childhood to adulthood, may be one of a school bully who seemed overwhelming and scary, but when you run into that same person today they may seem smaller and less intimidating, because both of you have changed. Maybe an adult you once knew to be strong and healthy, has aged or been sick to the point of frailty, consequently you look at them in a completely different way.

My point is this, depending how involved you are in something, and what you are comparing it to that determines the degree of difficulty. Sometimes our circumstance may seem overwhelming and intimidating, other times we feel we can handle it. We each draw on our respective resources through friends, family, personal faith, or even our finances, to give us strength or support handling unexpected circumstances, however long short or difficult that may be.

One analogy I like to use to give perspective of how we see things from a limited point of view, is this. Picture yourself, walking alone through woods on a moonless night holding only a small flashlight. The light can pierce the darkness, but for only a limited distance and direction. You can only make decisions for your walk based on the information gathered from what you see in that limited area.

Now picture yourself walking in the same area when the sun is directly overhead on a clear day. Even with the trees blocking some of the sun, you will be able to see clearly in all directions and for great distances. This allows you to make better decisions as to which direction to go, and gives confidence in your steps. How minor and even useless is that flashlight when you have the sun to guide you. I will only use the visual analogy here, because what I want you to understand, is the difference of what we see compared to what God sees.

Trials in life are similar to being alone and lost in some forest at night. Everything is unfamiliar and scary. We almost always start thinking of the worst possible outcome, believing our environment is working against us. Things we hear are multiplied in our minds because we do not understand them. Time drags as we wait in hopes of the situation turning positive.

Now think how much easier it would be if you were not alone. What if another person was with you for support, or better yet what if there were many people with you? It should be pretty obvious that the perspective might change from discouragement to encouragement, simply because of companionship.

The same encouragement can be true in respect to seeing things clearly, just like the sunlight dispersing the darkness. The more information we have to make decisions with, the more comfortable and confident we can be in making those difficult, life altering decisions.

One thing I can say for certain, nobody really understands the degree of hurt, misunderstanding, despair, or frustration one feels, unless they have actually experienced something of the same nature or close to it. An example of this is similar to a picture of a place you have never been. You see it, but have not experienced the sounds, smells, or any other emotions that may accompany what you see.

As a child I saw pictures of foreign countries and heard the stories of the culture differences, but until I actually took a mission trip to a third world country as a young adult, I did not fully understand or comprehend. I'll compare it to a roller coaster ride. Your friends tell you about the thrill of the first hill, how the stomach does not keep up with the rest of the body or the feeling you might fall off the ride. Only when you have experienced the coasters first hill yourself, can you relate to the thrill or agony it brings.

The roller coaster is another good example of the issues or hurts that life can bring. Once you are on and come over the top of the first hill, there is no getting off and you are going for the ride like it or not. Sometimes it's just a small roller coaster, and other times it's more than we can see, causing us to wonder if it will ever end.

Trials can have their ups and downs, and occasionally a sharp curve or two just like the roller coaster. Its good to know it will come to an end eventually, however even after the ride is over we still feel the effects. Just because whatever sidetracked you for whatever length of time seems done, the effects continue to have influence on us sometimes long after the hurt is past.

Usually difficulties, trials, or unplanned circumstances, create issues we did not previously think we would need to deal with on a personal basis. We always believe it happens only to the other guy, and we act surprised when we are the ones enduring hardships. Even if the trouble was a minor hiccup or speed bump in life, the wise realize they need to make adjustments to both allow these things, and be prepared to endure. It is very possible for someone to face the same difficulty again, and possibly to a greater degree.

It only seems reasonable we cannot remain the same after enduring hardships, because we should have matured through it and changed our perspective. I'm sure someone who has lost a loved one they genuinely cared for, will have a greater compassion for someone of similar pain. They have encountered and endured the same type of difficulty, gaining an understanding that can only be learned from experience, that's perspective.

It's been said the difference between a recession and depression, depends if you going through it or someone else is. Something may affect us while devastating others, such as a tornado ripping your neighbors house apart while the only damage you received were a few windows blown out. It does not take a genius to figure out it's only a speed bump for you, while your neighbor is dealing with a major disruption in life.

In the realm of perspective I wish to discuss time. Time plays a major part in how we handle issues in our lives. We are the now generation, impatient not wanting to wait for anything. Our society has not only taught us we can have things we desire immediately, but has also provided a way for it to happen. Some examples are, credit cards, fast food, ATMs, 24 hour fuel or food, the internet (anything from information to down loading movies and on line chats), microwave ovens, cell phones, I-pods, the list can go on with virtually everything instantly at our fingertips.

I need to inject a thought to ponder: I cannot find one time, that Jesus was in a hurry during his time on earth. Everything we call logical or might feel an obligation for, seemed to have no bearing on Christ. When the crowds came to hear him speak, he left them and went away alone to pray. When he was told Lazarus was dying he did not rush, but waited a few days actually letting him die. When the storm raged around him and his disciples, he slept in the boat.

In Samuel, we read the story of David the shepherd boy, who many years later, became king of Israel. In Genesis, we have the story of Joseph the younger brother who was sold into slavery, endured many years of uncertainty but was eventually promoted to second-in-command of the whole land of Egypt. Many years passed and many trials of difficult circumstances came into the lives of these two examples.

If you know the stories, you know it was not an easy road for either one of them, they probably even faced the same types of emotional anxieties you are subjected to. God gave us these examples in history to learn from, and be encouraged by.

The most important thing, most of us miss or neglect to acknowledge, is that whatever takes place in our lives just like in the lives of the biblical examples, is for the glory of God. We sometimes get wrapped up in our limited view of self-preservation.

I'm sure when Joseph sat in the Egyptian jail, he felt like it was the end of the line for him. It looked like a hopeless situation, but we know after spending years in jail God did have something special for him because he stayed faithful. Jesus himself did not start his ministry until he was thirty years old.

I point out these examples to illustrate, that we may not see the why we are enduring this particular crisis in our life. It may be many years, before you are able to use the present circumstance of learning and training. It takes many years for a fruit tree to grow from a seed into a mature productive tree. We need to look at our trials as training or maturing for a future opportunity to serve God.

Training is tough, it takes discipline and stretches us beyond what we are accustomed to. Self-discipline is the most difficult because we set our own agendas and limits. When it comes to life's difficult times, we don't always see them as training. We see them as some kind of discipline or misfortune, because we did not have control of the when how or what.

Training comes in different forms, depending on what we are being trained for. A runner trains different than a football player. An astronaut, banker, electrician, nurse, or fisherman, all require different types of training to be effective in their field or line of work. Whatever the particular issue anybody is being trained for, requires time.

Time is something we do not control. We cannot stop it, speed it up, slow it down, buy it, sell it, package it, or ignore it. Our trials, hurts, and undesirable circumstances are similar to time, we don't control them God does. We need to allow him to be the one we depend on to take us through it.

We have all heard that anything worthwhile takes time. During our time of training, even if it's not by our own choice, we need discipline and consistency or another way to put it is perseverance. Nobody goes into a project or race without knowing what or where the finish is. Life as it happens doesn't always allow us that privilege. However we can still set goals by making choices that keep us aimed in the right direction, regardless of what we may be facing or how long the duration of time is.

I have an example that may just help grasp a glimpse of how things might work out better for us, if we just let go of the control and work with God, instead of against him with our own ideas of how things should be.

Many of us have the privilege of driving a car, and with that privilege come a few rules of the road and personal responsibility. Those rules are for our own protection, even though we may feel they restrict our freedom. If someone decides they do not want to abide to the standard, they endanger not only themselves but others as well. If they disregard a stop sign or drive on the wrong side of the road, they may be lucky enough to get away with it for a while but the odds are not in their favor, continuing to disregard the law will eventually result in something drastic.

If a driver is caught breaking the law, they will or should be penalized, maybe even to the degree of losing the privilege of driving for a while. Although they may take the penalty as infringement on their rights or freedom, ultimately it is meant for good not only for them, but for the protection of others too.

God really does have our best interest in mind, even during those times we feel he has abandoned or forgotten us. We need to realize he sets limits for reasons that we cannot see or even understand, that could possibility have resulted in negative consequences if we had continued as we were.

I'm not suggesting that whatever you are going through is punishment, so please don't look at it that way. I am only suggesting you allow God to be your guide in life, especially during times of uncertainty.

I also believe we are not always enjoying the freedoms and blessings of Christ, because like the privilege of driving, we have our own ideas of how to handle things instead of trusting God. When your GPS gives you directions you may think you have a better way by choosing a shortcut that will save time, only to find out for some unexpected reason, you end up backtracking making the trip longer in the end.

If you knew the reward or blessing would equal or exceed your trial, would you have a different outlook while going through it? Galatians 6:9 "Let us not become weary in doing good, for in proper time we will reap a harvest if we do not give up". We get stuck in our narrow limited minds by drawing conclusions from what we see or understand. Perspective is going beyond where we are, looking at the whole picture instead of the temporary things that overwhelm us. Remember, perspective is how we view things in comparison.

INTRIGUING WORDS

Words are powerful. At some point in life, we hang onto every word someone is speaking, usually because it has a direct effect on us. The initial step of understanding how certain words influence our choices, is to understand their meaning and application.

Take the word insulate for instance. When something is insulated, it is protected from some outside force or environment. However the same word can be used to describe a place or person so removed from the normal routines of life, that it is almost impossible to get to it or them.

Personal barriers can sometimes keep the needed help from reaching us when needed. Our choices of being in control or insulating ourselves as a defense could possibly be prolonging the very situation we desire come to completion.

Lets be honest, when we hurt emotionally, words matter! However, most words spoken to us during the down times are usually not desired or received very well. We much rather be left alone, convinced that whomever is trying to be of some comfort to us knows nothing of the pain we are enduring.

Hurting people can and usually feel isolated or alone. The thought pattern is nobody knows how I feel, there is no hope, I can't take it, why me, this will never end, and nobody really cares about me anyway. Can you see or understand by the very thoughts of someone enduring difficult times, how they might feel as the emotions run wild? Maybe you are experiencing some of these thoughts at this very moment. May I suggest you are normal!

Don't despair or give up hope. I know the next phrase seems trite, but I know it's true. Things will change despite the darkness that surrounds and possibly even overwhelms you right now. You may even need to make adjustments that are rather difficult.

In Ecclesiastes 3:1 Solomon tells us, there is a time for everything, and a season for every activity under heaven. In verses 2-8 he continues to tell us about the different emotions and activities in life to which we are subjected. In verses 9-17 he comments on who we are compared to God and what our perspective should be. I challenge you to take your bible and read Ecclesiastes chapter three for yourself, and also suggest you conclude the reading with Ecclesiastes 12:13,14. This is where Solomon gives the summary of the wisdom he has acquired during life.

Sometimes it helps to think about the positive things we so often take for granted. Words spark memories and can bring instant relief or joy. Let me make some suggestions that may cause you at least for a few moments, to dwell on something other than what is presently dominating your thoughts. Let your mind wander as you think about the following phrases and the calming effect they may entice. Read them slowly, allow the thought to sink in.

Lightly falling rain, freshly mowed grass, flowers gently swaying in the breeze, birds singing, cloudless blue sky, the voice of a friend from far away, the smell of freshly baked bread, warm sunshine, the quietness of nature. As your mind thought on these few things, I would hope you could see how words can be a powerful tool, influencing not only thoughts, but attitude and emotions.

We can take every precaution known to man but we are still susceptible to such things as accidents, disease, sorrow, pain, disappointment, and ultimately death itself.

Sometimes we avoid people because we just want to be left alone, possibly for a good reason like being stressed out. We certainly don't want to offend someone during our time of irrational, sometimes legitimate thinking, at least that's a logical thought pattern, but in doing so we may have cheated ourselves of having a friend come alongside for support.

There are times when we try hiding from everything and or everybody. I'm not trying to justify this behavior, just merely acknowledge that it happens.

However, in reality we are actually saying, I can't and I won't deal with this, I don't need others, I want to wallow in my self pity, and I can handle this alone. The blunt truth is that it is not only selfish, but also a lonely path to personal destruction.

This is not the attitude God had in mind when he created us as relational beings. We need someone come beside to buffer or absorb, giving us support and encouragement when we face difficult situations. With the needed help we can actually say I can and I will. That help comes best from those who have experienced a similar disruption in life, that's why it's called a relationship. The word relationship means connection or similarity.

I wish to speak briefly about the word or the meaning behind the word tolerate. It simply means to put up with or accept. The application pertaining to tolerating can be from both sides of the hurt. The hurting individual really doesn't want help, or possibly doesn't know how to accept it so they tolerate it. The helping partner is likewise not sure how to help, or just feels obligated to be there so they also tolerate being there.

There is no benefit in tolerating. Its like spending an evening with someone and neither of you speak. Yes you are together and maybe that chases some of the loneliness or boredom away, but relationships take involvement, and communication is a major part of the connection. That communication is deeper than just being there or saying the right words, it is understanding and desiring to be the support or encouragement needed.

Hopefully you can see why it is so important to understand how the other person feels. Maybe you are able to make a connection on the same level, and help each other understand the feelings, emotions, questions, hopes, fears, or other issues that become relevant. The ultimately goal is that both sides desire and pursue the relationship to an ultimate level of working together, for the best possible outcome. Maybe that's why God allowed the situation to occur in the first place, so both of you can learn and mature through it.

If you are one who has already experienced a situation and you are aware of a brother or sister going through something similar, I believe God gives you the special privilege and responsibility, of being the one to come along side. In Matthew 25:40 Jesus declared: "Whatever you did for one of the least of these brothers of mine, you did for me."

Following are a few other words I wish to elaborate on that seem to be key issues. They are judged, self-esteem, dependent, worry, and contentment.

- Judged

The word judged brings a shutter to most people. We do not relish having others evaluate our lives, then drawing their own opinionated conclusions as to whether or not we have made the right decisions how to live life. Judged is one major aspect of how most people feel when going through one of lifes trials or difficulties.

If you are the helper, this is the one word or term to keep in your mind as a central focus while dealing with the hurting. Your words and your actions need to portray that you are not there to judge, but to come along side and to encourage. This is probably the biggest hinge point of winning their trust and being able to be part of the healing process. If you miss this important relationship-building tool, everything else will be surface quality only, because the hurting will write you off immediately.

To grasp my point, we must first understand what a judge is. A judge is one who has supreme authority to evaluate something such as a situation, character, contest, performance, behavior, or some competition, to conclude one final verdict or decision from multiple possibilities.

The way for a judge to draw the correct conclusion or verdict, is to see the whole picture with all the information and possibilities before making an informed decision, according to the laws or rules pertaining to the issue involved.

Why do we feel judged? Could it be because things did not work out as we planned, so we immediately pass judgment on ourselves? We believe we must have not been playing according to the rules and somehow cheated, or we took a shortcut and now are reaping our just reward. We reap what we sow, consequently we obviously must have done something wrong to bring this particular situation upon ourselves. We feel responsible for whatever we may have been involved in. Then we go the next step, beating ourselves up with personal evaluations or scenarios of what it was we did wrong. Sometimes it is of our own doing, we need not only be aware of that possibility but humble enough to admit it, asking for forgiveness and accepting the consequences of our actions.

Besides self-judging, we judge others. Before we do that, we need to ask ourselves a few questions. Do I know all the facts? Am I an expert in this area? Do I have the right? What if someone were judging me for something similar? I submit we stop spending our time and energy judging, instead we make effort to help or encourage.

- Self Esteem

A factor that tops the chart in a hurting persons life is self worth, or self esteem. When the plans we make and the goals we set come to a screeching halt because of some unforeseen or uncontrollable event, we have a natural tendency to look at ourselves as the main reason for the failure. It does not matter if it did or did not directly involve choices we made. We take it personal and somehow find a reason to blame ourselves. Sometimes the self-judgments are not due to the present circumstance, but what we failed to do prior to what is happening. Possibly not spending time with someone before they passed away, or not being who we should have been, affecting an outcome in someone else's life. Even taking advantage of someone or something, for a temporary personal gain only to see to late the impact it caused, exposing us for who we are.

Regardless of how we got to the point of judging ourselves for shortcomings and personal failures, we feel responsible and maybe rightfully so. If we can't control things we feel like useless pawns, convincing ourselves we are of no value, and therefore can't contribute anything positive to the world around us. Soon we quit trying and adopt the attitude of worthlessness to society.

Self-esteem or value, comes from seeing who we are from Gods point of view. Sometimes we make ourselves valuable by the worlds standards because of what we accomplish in society. Be it money, power, or status, our value is based only on the latest accomplishment. We are all subject to losing this kind of self worth at a moments notice. From the top there is plenty of room to fall, whether it is disrespect, personal humility, a lack of followers, or a loss of ability to persuade others we have the right answers. Society tells us our personal value comes from where we are in society, therefore giving us value or self worth by comparison.

Our real value comes from who we are, not what we do, have, or what others think. An interesting phase I have heard is: We are or become, what we think others think we are. That statement bothers me simply because if it were true, we have only assumed our identity according to what society allows us to be.

Our identity should be based on where we came from, our creator God! Our value is priceless. Each of us is unique and important as an individual. If someone is dedicated to your well-being, and cares about every aspect of your life, it doesn't take long for you to start believing it to the point of having self worth. God cares for you, and the people around you are the individuals God is using to show his love and concern for you personally.

- Dependent

Nobody likes having to depend on someone else to meet their basic needs of survival. We are naturally wired to be self-sufficient independent and in control of our own destiny. If we rely on others we feel they are in control, dominating our lives, making the decisions that directly affect who we are. We somehow get the idea that we will become what they want us to be, losing our own identity.

Maybe this is the reason we fight so hard, trying to maintain stability in our lives when it is disrupted by unexpected circumstance. We are full of pride - we sometimes call it integrity so we don't feel guilty. We think being dependent exposes us as weak, or below those around us. The opportunity we miss when we are absorbed in the attitude of poor me, is that others are not only able but willing to help us in difficult times.

Being dependent can have its rewards. Accept it, you may be pleasantly surprised. Maybe the one who comes along to help has some insight or ability to expedite recovery. What an opportunity to be a good example and possibly influence your helper in positive ways. You just might gain a friend through this whole ordeal too.

- Worry

Most people shy away from the word worry because it has a guilt factor attached. We all have been taught it is wrong to worry and by doing so we are not being spiritual. Lets be realistic, all normal people worry about something at sometime. I'm not trying to justify it but simply acknowledge worry as an emotion we entertain during times of uncertainty. We don't know how things may turn out, and as time or resources are running out, we begin to expect the worst. We start thinking the opportunity for improvement has vanished, especially when our prayers have seemingly gone unanswered.

Yes it is true worrying over something never changes it and giving it totally to God is the right answer. It is a fine line between running through the possible solutions and worry. Our prayers should be for Gods will, but we do not always know what that is, especially compared to what we believe the best answer is. God gave us the ability to think and make decisions and wants us to do so, but we must be careful not to cross over into the area of distress and anxiety. These are nothing less than symptoms of trying to take control of something we have no authority, ability, or right to.

- Contentment

Contentment is being satisfied with the way things are, happy and accepting of a situation or course of action. Not wanting to change anything from its present state, satisfied.

Everybody desires contentment. Isn't this what man longs for? We pursue it in many different ways, always trying to fill some need or want to give us the feeling that we have arrived. Contentment can only come from within, nobody else can decide for us if we are willing to accept things like they are in our lives.

God created families, with the idea of the parents taking the responsibility for teaching and providing the basic needs of their children. Humans sometimes do not measure up to the plans and principles God designed, but God will never fail his children. If we are under his watchful eye and he has our best interest in mind, shouldn't we be content, leaving no place for worry and anxiety? I know those are strong words and I wrestle with this concept just as much as you do. We all want the peace but have a hard time giving up the worry.

If nothing else has been learned by my own experience through the loss of income, it is that I can be very satisfied or content with a lot less of the materialistic things in life. When we strip away all the extra stuff in life and get down to the basics, we find where our real values lie. To help you grasp an understanding of this I will use an example that may not be so pleasant to some, but very direct in helping us better understand real value. For those going through physical pain, I apologize for using this type of example but I also know you will understand better than others may.

When we are healthy we set priorities as to what is important and how we spend or time and resources, but have you ever been so sick it consumes every part of your body? When that happens, you can think of nothing else. It doesn't matter if the lawn gets mowed, the dishes washed, or if you look presentable to anybody. You don't care about anything except feeling better. Maybe it's a stretch to see how this relates, but I wish to make the point of how priorities change and how the things we might normally see as having value, lose it in comparison to the present circumstance. What are the issues in your life keeping you from being content, happy, and satisfied?

Paul said in Philippians 4:11 "For I have learned to be content whatever the circumstances". I wish to point out Paul said he learned, it didn't just happen. I'm sure he had a few trials or difficulties in life which brought him to that point. We too must learn through our own not so pleasant experiences, to find contentment in what is of value to us.

NUTSHELL

In our on demanding world of getting what we want or need in days hours or minutes, I wish I could give you just a few right to the point, waste no time nuggets of advice. However it would be impossible for you to grasp the depth of what needs to be understood about lifes struggles. Hopefully as you have read through this book (shame on you last chapter readers) there have been a few eye opening, life applications and helpful truths to aid you along your journey.

We can't deny having feelings or emotions that dominate our thoughts when life drops out around us. So often we worry more about what others think, than what God does. Those feelings and emotions are there because we are confused, scared or have fear the unknown. Life has abruptly changed and can never have the carefree routine it previously held. History confirms that strength comes from, or is a result of adversity not compliance. As harsh as this may sound it's true. We don't really know who God is until God is our only option.

Pain and disappointment happens. As humans we want to avoid or ignore it, so a normal tendency is to do something that makes us feel good even if it is indulging in sin. It should be no surprise that we make the most important decisions in our lives during difficult times, simply because things have changed and we are forced to make choices to adapt. We choose to become better by giving of self or take the attitude of bitterness. The negative things that constantly knock you down are wearing you out, you are tired and want relief from the feeling of being stagnant or going backwards.

Don't let the evil of this world overwhelm or defeat you, remember as a believer you are a child of the king waiting for your faith to be sight. There is absolutely nothing this world can offer you that even comes close to the rewards of a person who pursuits God.. Even Jesus asked the question in Mark 8:36 "What good is it for a man to gain the whole world, yet forfeit his soul?"

The core of life is our relationship with God. If you do not know God on a personal basis, get a bible and read Romans 10:9-10 or Ephesians 2:8-9, they will tell you how to have that relationship and be sealed with Christ for all of eternity.

Following is a list to inspire your thoughts, while summing up what we need to focus on to move forward, after life has dwelt us the undesirable:

Dwell on the positive, be thankful in all things, pray for wisdom and endurance, allow God to be in control, pray for others taking the focus off yourself, never give up hope, sing praises, pray out loud and in the name of Jesus, expect answers, seek God, read his word, forgive, don't judge, be patient, let go of bitterness and envy, seek council, control your tongue, stop comparing yourself to others, love unconditionally, encourage others.

For those desiring to help the hurting I give the following. Loneliness and boredom are enemies, make effort to be a companion. Even when time has lapsed don't forget them, the odds are they are still in need of encouragement. Show genuine concern by listening and giving opinions only when asked. The personal touch of handshakes and hugs are appreciated. Use tender words when speaking. Never make them feel they are being judged or disciplined, but rather how important and valuable they are.

One observation I have had even while writing this book, is how many different things hinge on each other whether for the positive or the negative. I'm amazed how our emotions and personal choices influence not only our own lives, but have a lasting affect on those who are observing us. The observation and conclusion I suspect most are trying to make is, what relationship did that person have with Christ before, during, and after the trial? Is their relationship with God genuine or for some personal gain? They may make a decision about their own relationship with Christ, based on your example.

It matters not which side of the hurt you are on, you cannot remain the same if you are involved. The on the sidelines observer is the one who will lose the most by not gaining a friend, relationship, or personal growth. Yes you probably will make some mistakes, but we all learn by them and forgiveness is always possible if it is asked for with a truly repentant spirit.

Hopefully you have discovered by reading this book, how different words and some of their meanings, or how personal choices and the influence of others have major impacts on not only you, but also those around you. My goal was to show the many different ways self gets in the way and how we relate to each other as humans.

Once again, I will jog your memory by listing some words, and as you read through the list, try to verbally state their meanings and how it might influence an outcome from whatever side of hurt you are on.

Hurt, Mere Words, Council, Fear, Wisdom, Despair, Do's, Don'ts, Worry, Attitude, Loneliness, Compassion, Selfish, Judged, Frustrated, Avoid, Thankful, Understanding, Perspective, Confused, Tired, Valueless, Loved, Privileged, Stuff, Prayer, Action, Exposed, Relationships, Guilt, Comparison, Stagnant, Self Esteem, Relationships, Communication, Contentment, Training.

I know the list brings a lot of things to comprehend and analyze, but I also know these words can help you pinpoint where you are personally. If one or more of these words made you uncomfortable, I challenge you to figure out why and make any necessary adjustments in your life. We can only make adjustments and move on, when we discover what we are dealing with. Seek help and understanding before making decisions that can have lasting consequences or blessings.

Positive words and attitudes are what each of us desires to hear, or have for encouragement during the difficult times in life. Words like: Peace, joy, thankful, friend, loved, caring, and the reflective attitude that goes with them like: Smiles, listening ears, hugs, and giving of personal time to share the burden. Being thankful, I believe is not only a result of the right spirit and attitude, but reinforces or encourages each of us when we come to understand all the good things we experience, and how little we deserve.

If you are the hurting, suffering, discouraged or lonely, my prayer is for this be an encouraging start to a positive recovery. If you are the helper or encourager, I hope you may have gleaned some insight why those on the other side may feel and react to negative circumstances, not only allowing you to aid them but desiring to.

Hurting people want someone to physically come alongside in a nonjudgmental manner. Remember actions speak the loudest. You may not need to say anything, just being there is encouragement. It shows the other person they are important enough for you to interrupt your personal schedule.

Idle or misinterpreted words, can quickly cause the hurting person to shut you out in defense. If you come with an over bearing approach exclaiming something like: "What you really need to do". I guarantee it does not matter what you have to say beyond that initial statement because they are no longer listening to you. The proper way to help is in love, come along side as a support or with encouragement, not by pushing your own agenda or opinions. The only thing some have left in times of tribulation is their integrity, let them keep it, they are a person just like you.

They feel life has treated them unfairly, they are vulnerable, confused, exposed, and the emotions can run ahead of logic. Allow for these things, listen to them, let them know you care by your actions of attention and personal sacrifice of time, and maybe even personal resources. Don't avoid them or minimize their situation. Allow them the time it takes to work through the unsolicited disruption in life. Place yourself in their position, walk in their shoes.

How would you want others to respond to you if it were your trial?

Things happen for a reason, good and bad. Sometimes its because we reap what we sow. The bad things we reap because of our own actions are hard to swallow even if we do deserve it. The best we can do at that point is to admit our shortcomings, ask for forgiveness, then move on by learning from our mistakes and living with the consequences. We can't go back and certainly don't want to be stuck in some negative situation if we have the ability to get beyond it. So make the best choice after seeking council, take action by actively pursuing that choice.

Another reason things come into our lives may not be because of anything we did, but to help us grow or to glorify God through it. Our position is to accept and endure what has come our way, with the right attitude, spirit, and motivation.

As trite as this may sound when life has dealt you anything but pleasure, I'll risk saying it anyway because it is truth. Transformation within you, starts transformation around you. In other words, be the one who takes the first steps to new beginnings and a positive outlook! A life of meaning is the first step to a life of contentment.

Life is about personal choices. When hurt happens we choose to wallow in self-pity or use it for some purpose. I never suggested it was easy or the direction was clear. Whatever outcome and the ripple effect usually are a direct result of your choices and attitude.

Probably one of the biggest issues to deal with as a hurting person, is fear of the unknown. Uncertainty and lack of direction seem beyond reach when we need it the most. Not knowing what to expect or how to prepare for what is coming, creates additional stress at a difficult time.

My challenge to those desiring to help is this: If you have had an experience or similar trial, there is nobody better qualified than you to come along side of them, but only if you have the right attitude. From my own experience I can tell you, I really appreciated those who were blunt in the aspect of what to expect. Sugar coating and watering things down does not help the hurting prepare for what is ahead. The rest of you are not excused from being helpers just because you have not had that particular difficulty in life. God wants all of us to be, what we can, to whom we can, when we can.

The greatest ability is availability. We make the choice to get involved or not. Don't miss the opportunity to serve God when he makes it possible in your life. Remember who you are ultimately doing it for, and that God gives blessings to those who serve him with a willing heart.

Although you may be doing things to help others during their difficult time, it is very possible their struggle could help you in numerous ways too. Like strengthen your faith, build a relationship, give you purpose, keep you accountable, and maybe even find enjoyment or satisfaction in helping.

When the trial or difficulty seems to have ended, it hasn't. There are scars and possible changes in lifestyle that may never go away. When someone loses a loved one, the loneliness doesn't just stop. If a job loss or sickness has caused financial distress, it may take many years to dig back out. Continue to uphold or encourage those whose lives have been altered.

We all need each other at some time during life, regardless of how invincible and self sufficient we convince ourselves we are. I can't emphasize enough the principle of Matthew 7:12 which says: "So in everything, do to others what you would have them do to you." In our terminology, "Treat others the way you want to be treated". A strong push for helpers is Matthew 25:40 where Jesus said, "Whatever you did for the least of these brothers of mine, you did for me."

All these words mean nothing if we can't grasp or understand how to implement them. First we need to take a few steps back and seek council or wisdom. Wisdom is the ability to understand the accumulated information we have become aware of, and make sensible decisions or judgments accordingly. Taking the time and effort to gain understanding can save heartache later. When we have compared choices it gives a level of comfort and the determination to proceed with confidence.

Although most hurts that disrupt our lives are humiliating, a word of caution needs to be mentioned. Pride in the recovery process concerning our abilities can hinder us from maturing. Be careful your pride does not become your motivation, give credit where credit is due. The word JOY is a good example of what our position of service needs to be. Jesus Others Yourself, and in that order stands as a guide and reminder where we fit in while we have the privilege of living and serving with others for a few short years on this earth.

We all have memories of what we have done in the past. If they were negative or brought us personal feelings of failure or regret, we wish to forget them and bury them deep hoping never to relive the feelings again. The opposite should be true as we observe, learn and mature from the experience.

We also have positive memories to encourage us, especially those we come in contact with who have been good examples. May we have the ability to pull up those memories when we need the stamina, empowering us to press on and be the next generation to set a good example for those behind us. Pray with faith believing and expecting answers, not necessarily for what you want, but what benefits others or glorifies your maker.

Now for those who have read this book but are not the one hurting or experiencing some negative aspect of life at this time. Maybe you have never had to deal with anything in life that forced you to make a major change. It is also conceivable that right now you have brushed off most of what has been addressed as some over the top irrational pathetic one-sided opinion. Possibly even thinking someone just needs to pull themselves up by the bootstraps and accept life as it is. They need to move on without trying to get others to feel sorry for them.

Before you draw that conclusion, I challenge you to think of one person you may know who has had to, or is dealing with the most tragic situation any human has ever encountered. Then substitute yourself for that person asking what choices you would make, and how your emotions or feelings influence the outcome. At the present time you feel secure and unsusceptible to such demise, convincing yourself because of abilities or resources that it couldn't happen to you. Yes it can happen to you, life is unfair and disappointing in this world full of sin.

Until Christ returns to set things right or you are taken home to heaven, life can and will bring trouble or hurts to everybody at sometime. Our responsibility is to have the right attitude and motivation in all things, setting self aside for the glory of God.

Life is about choices. Most of us are capable of making intelligent choices. When life turns sour, you have been humiliated, things don't work the way you had planned, you will be faced with making choices. Remember relationships matter and whatever choices you make, will affect you and those around you for a very very long time. Consider the long-term benefits and consequences, and for whom you are living. Make every day count by having the right motivation along with the right attitude.

We live according to what we believe is true. Faith and hope, trump worry and fear every time.

There can be no better end to this book than three verses of challenge from the book of Philippians.

• Philippians 1:27 "Whatever happens, conduct yourselves in a manner worthy of the gospel of Christ."

• Philippians 4:11 "For I have learned to be content whatever the circumstance."

• Philippians 4:13 "I can do all things through him (Christ) who gives me strength."

Life is a journey, of which we know not the time
Plans of achievement, only the future will define
When life becomes senseless, Christ is there
Remember he came, your burdens to share
Be the fruit of the spirit, with love joy and peace
From binding sin, you will have great release
Peace patience kindness goodness and faith
Is the spirit of Gods heaven, just a small taste
Gentleness and self-control, against there is no law
Our comprehension of who God is, is so, so small
It takes a lifetime to learn, understand and grow
Choosing to live for, love, and our creator know
Believing there is an eternity for every soul
Well done, thou good and faithful servant
Are the sweetest words one could ever know
How will they remember you, what will they say?
I hope it's, you gave of self and sought God every day.

Scriptures taken from the Holy Bible, NIV Copyright 1973,1978,1984 by Bibilica Inc. Used by permission of Zondervan. All rights reserved worldwide.

All definitions are from: Microsoft Encarta College Dictionary. 1 ed. Microsoft St. Martins Press, 2001

www.ingramcontent.com/pod-product-compliance
Lightning Source LLC
LaVergne TN
LVHW010216070526
838199LV00062B/4606